CHOCOLATE CREAM PIE

Enjoy the Sweet Life With Chocolate

(A Highly Recommended Chocolate Dessert Cookbook)

Richard Whitlow

Published by Alex Howard

© Richard Whitlow

All Rights Reserved

Chocolate Cream Pie: Enjoy the Sweet Life With Chocolate (A Highly Recommended Chocolate Dessert Cookbook)

ISBN 978-1-990169-14-4

All rights reserved. No part of this guide may be reproduced in any form without permission in writing from the publisher except in the case of brief quotations embodied in critical articles or reviews.

Legal & Disclaimer

The information contained in this book is not designed to replace or take the place of any form of medicine or professional medical advice. The information in this book has been provided for educational and entertainment purposes only.

The information contained in this book has been compiled from sources deemed reliable, and it is accurate to the best of the Author's knowledge; however, the Author cannot guarantee its accuracy and validity and cannot be held liable for any errors or omissions. Changes are periodically made to this book. You must consult your doctor or get professional medical advice before using any of the suggested remedies, techniques, or information in this book.

Table of contents

PART 1 1

CHAPTER 1: THE CHOCOLATE SMOOTHIE WEIGHT-LOSS PROTOCOL 2

CHAPTER 2 CHOCOLATE AND GREENS SMOOTHIES 4

Chocolate Carrot & Spinach Smoothie 4
Chocolate Dandelion Greens And Green Tea Smoothie 5
Chocolate Lettuce Smoothie 5
Chocolate And Red Cabbage Smoothie 6
Chocolate Asparagus And Spinach Smoothie 6
Chocolate Hazelnut And Lettuce Smoothie 6
Chocolate Spinach And Macadamia Smoothie 7
Chocolate And Triple Greens Smoothie 7
Chocolate Beetroot And Asparagus Smoothie 8
Chocolate Cucumber And Swiss Chard Smoothie 8
Chocolate Spinach And Swiss Chard Lassi 9
Chocolate Almonds And Carrots Smoothie 9
Chocolate Spinach And Lettuce Smoothie 10
Chocolate Parsnips And Kale Smoothie 10
Chocolate And Turnip Greens Smoothie 11
Chocolate Beetroot And Lettuce Smoothie 11
Chocolate Broccoli And Spinach Lassi 12
Chocolate Blackberry And Kiwi Smoothie 12
Chocolate Swiss Chard And Watercress Smoothie 14
Chocolate Greens & Protein Smoothie 14

CHAPTER 3: CHOCOLATE AND FRUITS SMOOTHIES 15

Chocolate Mango Smoothie 15
Chocolate Peaches Lassi 15
Chocolate Raspberries And Strawberry Smoothie 16
Chocolate Blueberry Smoothie 16
Chocolate And Plum Smoothie 16
Chocolate Banana And Mint Smoothie 17
Chocolate Cherry Smoothie 17
Chocolate Peanut Butter And Berry Smoothie 18
Chocolate Cherry And Walnut Smoothie 18

Chocolate Apple Walnut Smoothie 19
Chocolate Strawberry And Orange Lassi 19
Chocolate Berries And Apricot Smoothie 20
Chocolate Peanut Butter And Grape Smoothie 20
Chocolate Almond Butter And Cherry Smoothie 21
Chocolate Peach And Nectarine Smoothie 21
Chocolate Raspberry And Lemon Smoothie 21
Chocolate Peanut Butter And Avocado Smoothie 22
Chocolate Avocado And Coconut Smoothie 22
Chocolate Avocado And Dates Smoothie 23
Chocolate Avocado And Berry Smoothie 23
Chocolate Kiwi And Pineapple Smoothie... 24

CHAPTER 4: CHOCOLATE FRUITS AND GREENS SMOOTHIES 25

Chocolaye Dates And Parsnip Smoothie 25
Chocolate Avocado And Spinach Smoothie 25
Chocolate Cherries And Mint Leaves Smoothie 26
Chocolate Plums And Mint Leaves Smoothie 26
Chocolate Mango And Lettuce Smoothie 27
Chocolate Spinach And Grape Smoothie 27
Chocolate Peanut Butter Kale And Date Smoothie 27
Chocolate Peaches Kale And Carrot Smoothie 28
Chocolate Dandelion Greens And Nectarine Smoothie 28
Chocolate Bell Pepper And Pear Smoothie 29
Chocolate Papaya And Bell Pepper Smoothie 29
Chocolate Dragon Fruit Spinach Green Tea Smoothie................................ 30
Chocolate Papaya Avocado And Kale Smoothie 30
Chocolate Grape And Collard Greens Smoothie 31
Chocolate Red Cabbage And Dragon Fruit Smoothie 31
Chocolate Cranberry And Lettuce Smoothie 32
Chocolate Dates And Lettuce Smoothie 32
Chocolate Pear And Bell Pepper Smoothie 33
Chocolate Cherry And Triple Bell Pepper Smoothie.................................... 33
Chocolate Watermelon And Lettuce Smoothie 34
Chocolate Watermelon And Cucumber Smoothie.. 34

CHAPTER 5: MEAL REPLACEMENT SMOOTHIES 36

CHOCOLATE COCONUT AND CUCUMBER SMOOTHIE 36
CHOCOLATE ORANGE AND SMOOTHIE 36
CHOCOLATE APRICOTS AND WATERMELON PROTEIN SMOOTHIE 37
CHOCOLATE CUCUMBER AND CABBAGE SMOOTHIE 37
CHOCOLATE LETTUCE AND RAISINS PROTEIN SMOOTHIE 38
CHOCOLATE PEANUT BUTTER PROTEIN SMOOTHIE 38
CHOCOLATE SPINACH AND COCONUT SMOOTHIE 39
CHOCOLATE AVOCADO AND DOUBLE GREEN PROTEIN SMOOTHIE 39
CHOCOLATE PEANUT BUTTER AND LETTUCE SMOOTHIE 40
CHOCOLATE PINEAPPLE AND MANGO PROTEIN SMOOTHIE 40
CHOCOLATE KALE AND MANGO PROTEIN SMOOTHIE 41
CHOCOLATE ORANGE AND MANGO PROTEIN LASSI 41
CHOCOLATE HAZELNUT GREEN TEA PROTEIN SMOOTHIE 43
CHOCOLATE DOUBLE BEAN GREEN TEA SMOOTHIE 43
CHOCOLATE COCONUT AND PEACHES PROTEIN SMOOTHIE 44
CHOCOLATE NECTARINE PROTEIN SMOOTHIE 44
CHOCOLATE APRICOT AND GRAPEFRUIT PROTEIN SMOOTHIE 45
CHOCOLATE BELL PEPPER PROTEIN SMOOTHIE 45
CHOCOLATE CITRUS AND PROTEIN LASSI 46
CHOCOLATE KALE AND PROTEIN SMOOTHIE 46
CHOCOLATE PEANUT BUTTER AND APPLE PROTEIN LASSI 46

CHAPTER 6: CHEAT DAY SMOOTHIES 48

CHOCOLATE GRAPE SMOOTHIE 48
CHOCOLATE PEANUT BUTTER AND HAZELNUT SMOOTHIE 48
CHOCOLATE MINT SMOOTHIE 49
CHOCOLATE PECAN AND MACADAMIA SMOOTHIE 49
DOUBLE CHOCOLATE AND PEANUT BUTTER SMOOTHIE 50
CHOCOLATE BLUEBERRY SMOOTHIE 50
CHOCOLATE PEACH AND MANGO SMOOTHIE 51
CHOCOLATE PEACHES AND DATE SMOOTHIE 51
CHOCOLATE PINEAPPLE AND KIWI SMOOTHIE 51
CHOCOLATE AVOCADO AND MANGO SMOOTHIE 52
CHOCOLATE NUTELLA AND PEANUT BUTTER SMOOTHIE 52
CHOCOLATE RED BEAN SMOOTHIE 53
WHITE CHOCOLATE MACADAMIA AND CHERRY SMOOTHIE 53

WHITE CHOCOLATE GREEN TEA SMOOTHIE	54
CHOCOLATE PURPLE SMOOTHIE	54
CHOCOLATE ALMONDS AND PEACHES SMOOTHIE	55
CHOCOLATE COOKIE BUTTER SMOOTHIE	55
CHOCOLATE AVOCADO AND MACADAMIA GREEN TEA SMOOTHIE	56
CHOCOLATE COCONUT AND TROPICAL FRUIT SMOOTHIE	56
WHITE CHOCOLATE RAISIN SMOOTHIE	57
CHOCOLATE AVOCADO AND NECTARINE SMOOTHIE	57
DARK CHOCOLATE & SEA SALT COOKIES	58
CARAMEL PECAN CINNAMON ROLL COOKIES	59
GHIRARDELLI BLACK & WHITES	60
CHOCOLATE CHIPPED GRANOLA COOKIES	61
CINNAMON & WHITE CHOCOLATE COOKIES	62
CHOCOLATE CHIP COOKIES 1.0	63
GRANDMA'S CHOCO-CHIP DELIGHTS	64
BANANA-APPLE CHOCOLATE CHUNK COOKIES	66
FRECKLES 'N BUMPS	67
PASSOVER CHOCOLATE-CHIP COOKIES	68
MINNESOTA'S FAVORITE COOKIE	69
KITCHEN-SINK COOKIES	70
DOUBLE CHOCOLATE MINT COOKIES	71
ALMOND CHOCOLATE & COCONUT COOKIES	72
LODGE COOKIES	72
CHOCOLATE DOODLES	74
SCOOTER'S CHEWY CHOCOLATE COOKIES	74
TRIPLE CHOCOLATE CHUNK-O COOKIE	75
MAKING 3 CHOCOLATE GLAZE:	76
JIMMY'S CHOCOLATE CHIP COOKIES	76
CHOCOLATE MACAROONS	77
MEGAN'S CHOCOLATE CHIP OATMEAL COOKIES	78
GIANT CRISP CHOCOLATE CHIP COOKIES	78
WHITE CHOCOLATE &MACADAMIA NUT	79
CHOCOLATE CHIP COOKIES (GLUTEN FREE)	80
ALL TIME GREAT CHOCOLATE CHIP COOKIE	81
AMERICA'S BEST CHOCOLATE CHIP COOKIES	82
PEANUT-BUTTER CHEWS	83

ADAM'S DIRT COOKIES 84
CHOCOLATE CHIP PEPPERMINT COOKIES 85
EGG FREE CHOCOLATE CHIP PUMPKIN COOKIES 86
CAKE MIX COOKIES 86
AWARD WINNING SOFT CHOCOLATE CHIP COOKIES 87
BEST CHOCOLATE CHIP COOKIES 88
PUFFY CHOCOLATY CHIP COOKIES 89
ABSOLUTELY EXCELLENT OATMEAL COOKIES 89
CHOCOLATY MARSHMALLOW COOKIES 90
CHERRY MOUNTAIN CHOCOLATE COOKIES 91
BEST BIG, FAT, CHEWY CHOCOLATE CHIP COOKIE 93
CHOCOLATE JUMBO 94
MAGGIE'S CAMPER SPECIALS 94
KILLER CHOCOLATE CHIP COOKIE 95
DR. GOODCOOKIE 96
NO PEEKING! 97
CHEWY CHOCOLATE CHIP OATMEAL COOKIES 98
CHOCOLATY CHOCOLATE CHIP COOKIES 1.0 99

PART 2 101

INTRODUCTION 102

ULTIMATE DARK CHOCOLATE CAKE 103

OOZING CHOCOLATE LAVA CAKE 105
CHOCOLATE AND COFFEE CAKE 107
EASY DARK CHOCOLATE CAKE 109
CHOCOLATE MOUSSE CAKE 111
APPLE AND CHOCOLATE CAKE 113
CHOCOLATE MOCHA CAKE 115
FLOURLESS CHOCOLATE CAKE 117
CHOCOLATE BUNDT CAKE WITH RASPBERRIES 119
MOIST AND RICH CHOCOLATE CUPCAKE 121
HEAVENLY BROWNIES 123
HOMEMADE CHOCOLATE SOUFFLÉ 125

SUMPTUOUS CHOCOLATE BLANCMANGE 127

CHOCO PROFITEROLES 129

Easy Rocky Road Bars 131
Chocolate And Hazelnut Ice Cream 133
Homemade Double Chocolate Ice Cream 135
Homemade Chocolate Chip Energy Bars 137

THE ULTIMATE CHOCOLATE MOUSSE 139

Chocolate And Raspberry Mini Tarts 141
Strawberries Dipped In Chocolate 143
Delightful Chocolate Truffles 144
Chocolate And Marshmallow Fudge Bars 146
Classic And Easy Chocolate Pie 148
Chocolate Pancakes 150
Easy Homemade Chocolate Crinkles 152
Mini Chocolate And Peanut Butter Cups 154
Chocolate Oatmeal Porridge 156
Almond And Chocolate-Covered Biscuit Sticks 158
Chocolate Pavlova 160
Banana Choco Pops 162
Homemade S'mores 164
Chocolate Fudge Bars 165
Chocolate-Covered Cherry Bites 167
Choco Peppermint Bites 169
Chocolate Bubble Tea 171
Hot Chocolate With Marshmallows 172
Cinnamon-Spiced Hot Chocolate 174
Rich Chocolate Milkshake 176
Cookies And Cream Shake 177
Chocolate And Vanilla Smoothie 178
Chocolate And Banana Smoothie 180
White Chocolate Mocha Drink 182
Chocolate Almond Tea Latte 183
Caramel Hot Chocolate 185

Part 1

Chapter 1: The Chocolate Smoothie Weight-loss Protocol

Before you start this program, here are some of the things that you need to remember with your diet.
1.) You need to eat less than what your body burns on a daily basis.
2.) Your diet has to have a good amount of fiber.
3.) It needs to be sustainable.
Having chocolate smoothies can help you with these 3. This guide is divided into several chapters. Chapter 2 deals with chocolate & greens smoothies. You can use the smoothies in this chapter 4-5 days a week.
Chapter 3 deals with the fruit smoothies and you can use the smoothies in this chapter 1-2 times a week. Chapter 4 deals with chocolate vegetable and fruit smoothies. You can use the smoothies in this chapter 2-3 times a week.
Chapter 5 deals with meal replacement smoothies. You can use the smoothies in this chapter to replace your meals and keep yourself at a caloric deficit throughout the day while getting the necessary macronutrients. You can make these smoothies 2-3 times a week or whenever you feel like you can't get a decent healthy meal that day.
Chapter 6 deals with the cheat day smoothies. These are the smoothies that you make only once a week. Keep in mind that these smoothies are loaded with calories.
For the majority of this book, we'll be using cocoa to make our chocolate smoothies. The good news is that good cocoa contains almost all of the flavors of dark chocolate without the fat and calories. Make sure to buy a good brand of cocoa.
We'll be using Dutch-processed Cocoa because it has a smoother texture and it dissolves easily. Some of the good brands are E. Guittard or Barry Callebaut Extra Brute. You can also use regular cocoa as well. A good brand of regular cocoa that I usually

recommend to my students is Ghirardelli. Just remember that your cocoa doesn't have to be pricey. It just has to be something that you love to drink.

Chapter 2 Chocolate and Greens Smoothies

Chocolate Carrot & Spinach Smoothie

Ingredients:
1 cup Almond Milk, unsweetened
½ cup Baby Spinach, coarsely chopped
1/4 cup Parsnips, peeled and chopped
1/4 cup Carrots, peeled and chopped
2 tbsp. Dutch-processed Cocoa
Ice

Steps:
1.) Blend the leafy greens & liquids first at low speed for 1 min.
2.) Add the fruits & the rest of the ingredients. Blend at slow speed for 1 min.
3.) Move to medium speed until you see a vortex continue blending for 1 min.
4.) Blend at high speed for 1 min.

Chocolate Dandelion Greens And Green Tea Smoothie

Ingredients:
1 Cup Unsweetened Almond Milk
¼ cup Matcha Green Tea Powder
¾ cup Dandelion Greens, coarsely chopped
4 ½ tsp. Dutch-processed Cocoa
1/4 cup Parsnips, peeled and chopped

Steps:
1.) Blend the leafy greens & liquids first at low speed for 1 min.
2.) Add the fruits & the rest of the ingredients. Blend at slow speed for 1 min.
3.) Move to medium speed until you see a vortex continue blending for 1 min.
4.) Blend at high speed for 1 min.

Chocolate Lettuce Smoothie

Ingredients:
1 Cup Unsweetened Almond Milk
½ Cup Ice Berg Lettuce
¼ cup Parsnips, peeled and chopped
¼ cup Romaine Lettuce
1 tbsp. Dutch-processed Cocoa

Steps:
1.) Blend the leafy greens & liquids first at low speed for 1 min.
2.) Add the fruits & the rest of the ingredients. Blend at slow speed for 1 min.
3.) Move to medium speed until you see a vortex continue blending for 1 min.
4.) Blend at high speed for 1 min.

Chocolate And Red Cabbage Smoothie
Ingredients:
½ Cup Coconut Milk
½ Cup Milk
¼ Cup Red Cabbage, coarsely chopped
1/3 cup Parsnips, peeled and chopped
¼ cup Broccoli florets, coarsely chopped
2 tbsp. Dutch-processed Cocoa
Steps:
1.) Blend the leafy greens & liquids first at low speed for 1 min.
2.) Add the fruits & the rest of the ingredients. Blend at slow speed for 1 min.
3.) Move to medium speed until you see a vortex continue blending for 1 min.
4.) Blend at high speed for 1 min.

Chocolate Asparagus And Spinach Smoothie
Ingredients:
1 Cup Fresh Lemon Juice
½ Cup Baby Spinach Leaves, coarsely chopped
1/4 cup Parsnips, peeled and chopped
1/3 Cup Asparagus Spears, coarsely chopped
2 tbsp. Dutch-processed Cocoa
Steps:
1.) Blend the leafy greens & liquids first at low speed for 1 min.
2.) Add the fruits & the rest of the ingredients. Blend at slow speed for 1 min.
3.) Move to medium speed until you see a vortex continue blending for 1 min.
4.) Blend at high speed for 1 min.

Chocolate Hazelnut And Lettuce Smoothie
Ingredients:
1 Cup Milk

¼ cup Parsnips, peeled and chopped
¼ Cup Hazelnut, finely ground
¼ Cup Ice Berg Lettuce
¼ Cup Carrots, coarsely chopped
1 tbsp. Peanut Butter
4 ½ tsp. Dutch-processed Cocoa

Steps:
1.) Blend the leafy greens & liquids first at low speed for 1 min.
2.) Add the fruits & the rest of the ingredients. Blend at slow speed for 1 min.
3.) Move to medium speed until you see a vortex continue blending for 1 min.
4.) Blend at high speed for 1 min.

Chocolate Spinach And Macadamia Smoothie

Ingredients:
1 cup Unsweetened Almond Milk
1 Tbsp Macadamia Nut Oil
2/3 Cup Baby Spinach Leaves, coarsely chopped
1/4 cup Parsnips, peeled and chopped
2 tbsp. Dutch-processed Cocoa

Steps:
1.) Blend the leafy greens & liquids first at low speed for 1 min.
2.) Add the fruits & the rest of the ingredients. Blend at slow speed for 1 min.
3.) Move to medium speed until you see a vortex continue blending for 1 min.
4.) Blend at high speed for 1 min.

Chocolate And Triple Greens Smoothie

Ingredients:
1 Cup Coconut Water
¼ cup Parsnips, peeled and chopped
¼ Cup Dandelion Greens

¼ cup Baby Spinach Leaves
¼ cup Kale, coarsely chopped
2 tbsp. peanut butter
4 ½ tsp. Dutch-processed Cocoa

Steps:
1.) Blend the leafy greens & liquids first at low speed for 1 min.
2.) Add the fruits & the rest of the ingredients. Blend at slow speed for 1 min.
3.) Move to medium speed until you see a vortex continue blending for 1 min.
4.) Blend at high speed for 1 min.

Chocolate Beetroot And Asparagus Smoothie

Ingredients:
1 Cup Unsweetened Almond Milk
½ Cup Beetroot
¼ Cup Asparagus
¼ cup Parsnips, peeled and chopped
4 ½ tsp. Dutch-processed Cocoa

Steps:
1.) Blend the leafy greens & liquids first at low speed for 1 min.
2.) Add the fruits & the rest of the ingredients. Blend at slow speed for 1 min.
3.) Move to medium speed until you see a vortex continue blending for 1 min.
4.) Blend at high speed for 1 min.

Chocolate Cucumber And Swiss Chard Smoothie

Ingredients:
1 Cup Low-fat Milk
2 Tbsp. Walnut Oil
½ cup Swiss Chard
½ medium cucumber, peeled and sliced

1/4 cup Parsnips, peeled and chopped
¼ cup mint leaves, coarsely chopped
2 tbsp. Dutch-processed Cocoa
5-6 Ice Cubes

Steps:
1.) Blend the leafy greens & liquids first at low speed for 1 min.
2.) Add the fruits & the rest of the ingredients. Blend at slow speed for 1 min.
3.) Move to medium speed until you see a vortex continue blending for 1 min.
4.) Blend at high speed for 1 min.

Chocolate Spinach And Swiss Chard Lassi

Ingredients:
1 Cup Unsweetened Almond Milk
½ Cup Greek Yogurt
1/3 cup Parsnips, peeled and chopped
½ Cup Swiss Chard
½ Cup Baby Spinach Leaves, Coarsely chopped
2 tbsp. Dutch-processed Cocoa

Steps:
1.) Blend the leafy greens & liquids first at low speed for 1 min.
2.) Add the fruits & the rest of the ingredients. Blend at slow speed for 1 min.
3.) Move to medium speed until you see a vortex continue blending for 1 min.
4.) Blend at high speed for 1 min.

Chocolate Almonds And Carrots Smoothie

Ingredients:
1 Cup Unsweetened Almond Milk
¼ cup Almonds, finely ground
¼ tsp. Cinnamon

¼ cup Parsnips, peeled and chopped
¼ cup Carrots
1 tbsp. Dutch-processed Cocoa

Steps:
1.) Blend the leafy greens & liquids first at low speed for 1 min.
2.) Add the fruits & the rest of the ingredients. Blend at slow speed for 1 min.
3.) Move to medium speed until you see a vortex continue blending for 1 min.
4.) Blend at high speed for 1 min.

Chocolate Spinach And Lettuce Smoothie

Ingredients:
1 Cup Low-fat Milk
1/3 Cup Baby Spinach, coarsely chopped
1/3 Cup Romaine Lettuce
1/4 cup Parsnips, peeled and chopped
1 tbsp. Dutch-processed Cocoa

Steps:
1.) Blend the leafy greens & liquids first at low speed for 1 min.
2.) Add the fruits & the rest of the ingredients. Blend at slow speed for 1 min.
3.) Move to medium speed until you see a vortex continue blending for 1 min.
4.) Blend at high speed for 1 min.

Chocolate Parsnips And Kale Smoothie

Ingredients:
1 ¼ Cup Unsweetened Almond Milk
½ Cup Kale, stems removed and coarsely chopped
1/4 cup Parsnips, peeled and chopped
4 ½ tsp. Dutch-processed Cocoa

Steps:

1.) Blend the leafy greens & liquids first at low speed for 1 min.
2.) Add the fruits & the rest of the ingredients. Blend at slow speed for 1 min.
3.) Move to medium speed until you see a vortex continue blending for 1 min.
4.) Blend at high speed for 1 min.

Chocolate And Turnip Greens Smoothie

Ingredients:
1 Cup Almond Milk
¼ cup Parsnips, peeled and chopped
¼ cup Beet Root
¼ cup Baby Spinach Leaves
¼ cup Turnip Greens, coarsely chopped
4 ½ tsp. Dutch-processed Cocoa

Steps:
1.) Blend the leafy greens & liquids first at low speed for 1 min.
2.) Add the fruits & the rest of the ingredients. Blend at slow speed for 1 min.
3.) Move to medium speed until you see a vortex continue blending for 1 min.
4.) Blend at high speed for 1 min.

Chocolate Beetroot And Lettuce Smoothie

Ingredients:
1 Cup Coconut Milk
1/4 cup Parsnips, peeled and chopped
¼ Cup Romaine Lettuce
¼ tsp. ground ginger
¼ cup Beet Root
2 tbsp. Dutch-processed Cocoa

Steps:
1.) Blend the leafy greens & liquids first at low speed for 1 min.

2.) Add the fruits & the rest of the ingredients. Blend at slow speed for 1 min.
3.) Move to medium speed until you see a vortex continue blending for 1 min.
4.) Blend at high speed for 1 min.

Chocolate Broccoli And Spinach Lassi

Ingredients:
1 Cup Plain Yogurt
1/4 cup Parsnips, peeled and chopped
½ cup Broccoli florets, coarsely chopped
¼ cup Cauliflower florets, coarsely chopped
¼ cup Baby Spinach Leaves, coarsely chopped
2 tbsp. Dutch-processed Cocoa
5-6 Ice Cubes

Steps:
1.) Blend the leafy greens & liquids first at low speed for 1 min.
2.) Add the fruits & the rest of the ingredients. Blend at slow speed for 1 min.
3.) Move to medium speed until you see a vortex continue blending for 1 min.
4.) Blend at high speed for 1 min.

Chocolate Blackberry And Kiwi Smoothie

Ingredients:
1 Cup Milk
1 tbsp. Dutch-processed cocoa powder
1/4 cup Parsnips, peeled and chopped
½ cup Collard Greens, coarsely chopped
¼ cup Romaine Lettuce, coarsely chopped
5-6 Ice Cubes

Steps:
1.) Blend the leafy greens & liquids first at low speed for 1 min.

2.) Add the fruits & the rest of the ingredients. Blend at slow speed for 1 min.
3.) Move to medium speed until you see a vortex continue blending for 1 min.
4.) Blend at high speed for 1 min.

Chocolate Swiss Chard And Watercress Smoothie

Ingredients:
1 Cup Almond Milk
¼ cup Parsnips, peeled and chopped
½ Cup Swiss Chard
¼ cup watercress
2 tbsp. Dutch-processed Cocoa

Steps:
1.) Blend the leafy greens & liquids first at low speed for 1 min.
2.) Add the fruits & the rest of the ingredients. Blend at slow speed for 1 min.
3.) Move to medium speed until you see a vortex continue blending for 1 min.
4.) Blend at high speed for 1 min.

Chocolate Greens & Protein Smoothie

Ingredients:
1 Cup Milk
¼ cup canned Chickpeas or Garbanzo Beans, coarsely chopped
1/3 cup broccoli florets, coarsely chopped
¼ cup Canned Red Kidney Beans, rinsed and drained
1/4 cup Parsnips, peeled and chopped
4 ½ tsp. Dutch-processed Cocoa
1 tbsp. whey protein
4-5 Ice Cubes

Steps:
1.) Blend the leafy greens & liquids first at low speed for 1 min.
2.) Add the fruits & the rest of the ingredients. Blend at slow speed for 1 min.
3.) Move to medium speed until you see a vortex continue blending for 1 min.
4.) Blend at high speed for 1 min.

Chapter 3: Chocolate and Fruits Smoothies

Chocolate Mango Smoothie

Ingredients:
¼ Cup Oats
1 Cup Coconut Water
2 Tbsp. Dutch-processed Cocoa
½ cup Mango, pitted and sliced
½ medium banana (optional)
5-6 Ice Cubes

Steps:
1.) Blend the leafy greens & liquids first at low speed for 1 min.
2.) Add the fruits & the rest of the ingredients. Blend at slow speed for 1 min.
3.) Move to medium speed until you see a vortex continue blending for 1 min.
4.) Blend at high speed for 1 min.

Chocolate Peaches Lassi

Ingredients:
1 Cup Yogurt
¼ cup Peaches
2 tbsp. Dutch-processed Cocoa
¾ cup Strawberries, sliced
5-6 Ice Cubes

Steps:
1.) Blend the leafy greens & liquids first at low speed for 1 min.
2.) Add the fruits & the rest of the ingredients. Blend at slow speed for 1 min.
3.) Move to medium speed until you see a vortex continue blending for 1 min.
4.) Blend at high speed for 1 min.

Chocolate Raspberries And Strawberry Smoothie

Ingredients:
1 Cup Almond Milk
2 tbsp. Dutch-processed Cocoa
¾ Cup Raspberries
¼ cup Strawberries

Steps:
1.) Blend the leafy greens & liquids first at low speed for 1 min.
2.) Add the fruits & the rest of the ingredients. Blend at slow speed for 1 min.
3.) Move to medium speed until you see a vortex continue blending for 1 min.
4.) Blend at high speed for 1 min.

Chocolate Blueberry Smoothie

Ingredients:
1 Cup Grape Juice
¾ Cup Blueberries
2 tbsp. Dutch-processed Cocoa
¼ cup Unsweetened Almond Milk

Steps:
1.) Blend the leafy greens & liquids first at low speed for 1 min.
2.) Add the fruits & the rest of the ingredients. Blend at slow speed for 1 min.
3.) Move to medium speed until you see a vortex continue blending for 1 min.
4.) Blend at high speed for 1 min.

Chocolate And Plum Smoothie

Ingredients:
1 Cup Coconut water
½ cup Plums
¼ Cup Oats
2 tbsp. Dutch-processed Cocoa

1 medium banana, sliced
4-5 Ice Cubes

Steps:
1.) Blend the leafy greens & liquids first at low speed for 1 min.
2.) Add the fruits & the rest of the ingredients. Blend at slow speed for 1 min.
3.) Move to medium speed until you see a vortex continue blending for 1 min.
4.) Blend at high speed for 1 min.

Chocolate Banana And Mint Smoothie

Ingredients:
1 Cup Almond Milk
¼ Hazelnuts, finely ground
¾ cup 2 tbsp. Dutch-processed Cocoa
1 medium Banana, coarsely chopped
¼ cup mint leaves coarsely chopped
4-5 Ice Cubes

Steps:
1.) Blend the leafy greens & liquids first at low speed for 1 min.
2.) Add the fruits & the rest of the ingredients. Blend at slow speed for 1 min.
3.) Move to medium speed until you see a vortex continue blending for 1 min.
4.) Blend at high speed for 1 min.

Chocolate Cherry Smoothie

Ingredients:
1 Cup Low-fat Milk
½ medium banana, sliced
½ Cup Cherries, Pitted and Coarsely Chopped
2 tbsp. Dutch-processed Cocoa
4-5 Ice Cubes

Steps:
1.) Blend the leafy greens & liquids first at low speed for 1 min.
2.) Add the fruits & the rest of the ingredients. Blend at slow speed for 1 min.
3.) Move to medium speed until you see a vortex continue blending for 1 min.
4.) Blend at high speed for 1 min.

Chocolate Peanut Butter And Berry Smoothie

Ingredients:
1 Cup Unsweetened Almond Milk
½ cup Strawberries
¼ cup Raspberries
½ cup 2 tbsp. Dutch-processed Cocoa
1 Tbsp. Peanut Butter
1 medium Banana, sliced

Steps:
1.) Blend the leafy greens & liquids first at low speed for 1 min.
2.) Add the fruits & the rest of the ingredients. Blend at slow speed for 1 min.
3.) Move to medium speed until you see a vortex continue blending for 1 min.
4.) Blend at high speed for 1 min.

Chocolate Cherry And Walnut Smoothie

Ingredients:
1 Cup Milk
2 tbsp. Dutch-processed Cocoa
¼ Cup Walnuts, finely ground
½ Cup Cherries, pitted and coarsely chopped
½ tsp. Mint Extract

Steps:
1.) Blend the leafy greens & liquids first at low speed for 1 min.

2.) Add the fruits & the rest of the ingredients. Blend at slow speed for 1 min.
3.) Move to medium speed until you see a vortex continue blending for 1 min.
4.) Blend at high speed for 1 min.

Chocolate Apple Walnut Smoothie

Ingredients:
1 Cup Almond Milk
2 tbsp. Dutch-processed Cocoa
½ cup Apple
¼ Cup Walnuts, finely ground
½ tsp. cinnamon
4-5 Ice Cubes

Steps:
1.) Blend the leafy greens & liquids first at low speed for 1 min.
2.) Add the fruits & the rest of the ingredients. Blend at slow speed for 1 min.
3.) Move to medium speed until you see a vortex continue blending for 1 min.
4.) Blend at high speed for 1 min.

Chocolate Strawberry And Orange Lassi

Ingredients:
1 Cup Yogurt
2 tbsp. Dutch-processed Cocoa
½ cup Strawberries, sliced
¼ Cup Orange, deseeded and peeled
1 medium banana

Steps:
1.) Blend the leafy greens & liquids first at low speed for 1 min.
2.) Add the fruits & the rest of the ingredients. Blend at slow speed for 1 min.
3.) Move to medium speed until you see a vortex continue blending for 1 min.

4.) Blend at high speed for 1 min.

Chocolate Berries And Apricot Smoothie

Ingredients:
1 Cup Ice Cold Water
¼ Cup Apricots, pitted and sliced
2 tbsp. Dutch-processed Cocoa
¼ cup Blueberries, coarsely chopped
5-6 Ice Cubes
Steps:
1.) Blend the leafy greens & liquids first at low speed for 1 min.
2.) Add the fruits & the rest of the ingredients. Blend at slow speed for 1 min.
3.) Move to medium speed until you see a vortex continue blending for 1 min.
4.) Blend at high speed for 1 min.

Chocolate Peanut Butter And Grape Smoothie

Ingredients:
1 Cup Unsweetened Almond Milk
2 tbsp. Dutch-processed Cocoa
¼ Cup Grapes, deseeded and coarsely chopped
2 tbsp. Peanut Butter
1 tbsp. Dutch-processed Cocoa Powder
5-6 Ice Cubes
Steps:
1.) Blend the leafy greens & liquids first at low speed for 1 min.
2.) Add the fruits & the rest of the ingredients. Blend at slow speed for 1 min.
3.) Move to medium speed until you see a vortex continue blending for 1 min.
4.) Blend at high speed for 1 min.

Chocolate Almond Butter And Cherry Smoothie

Ingredients:
1 Cup Unsweetened Almond Milk
¼ Cup Cherries, pitted and sliced
2 tbsp. Dutch-processed Cocoa
2 tbsp. Almond Butter
¼ cup oats
1 large Banana, frozen
Steps:
1.) Blend the leafy greens & liquids first at low speed for 1 min.
2.) Add the fruits & the rest of the ingredients. Blend at slow speed for 1 min.
3.) Move to medium speed until you see a vortex continue blending for 1 min.
4.) Blend at high speed for 1 min.

Chocolate Peach And Nectarine Smoothie

Ingredients:
1 Cup Coconut water
¼ cup Peach
¼ Cup Nectarines
½ Cup Cashew Nuts, finely ground
2 tbsp. Dutch-processed cocoa
Steps:
1.) Blend the leafy greens & liquids first at low speed for 1 min.
2.) Add the fruits & the rest of the ingredients. Blend at slow speed for 1 min.
3.) Move to medium speed until you see a vortex continue blending for 1 min.
4.) Blend at high speed for 1 min.

Chocolate Raspberry And Lemon Smoothie

Ingredients:

1 Cup Almond Milk Unsweetened
2 tbsp. Dutch-processed Cocoa
¼ cup raspberries
1 tbsp. Olive Oil
1 tsp. lemon zest
4-5 Ice Cubes

Steps:
1.) Blend the leafy greens & liquids first at low speed for 1 min.
2.) Add the fruits & the rest of the ingredients. Blend at slow speed for 1 min.
3.) Move to medium speed until you see a vortex continue blending for 1 min.
4.) Blend at high speed for 1 min.

Chocolate Peanut Butter And Avocado Smoothie

Ingredients:
1 Cup Ice Cold Water
½ cup 2 tbsp. Dutch-processed Cocoa
½ medium Banana, sliced
2 tbsp. Peanut Butter
¼ cup Avocado, pitted and sliced
4-5 Ice Cubes

Steps:
1.) Blend the leafy greens & liquids first at low speed for 1 min.
2.) Add the fruits & the rest of the ingredients. Blend at slow speed for 1 min.
3.) Move to medium speed until you see a vortex continue blending for 1 min.
4.) Blend at high speed for 1 min.

Chocolate Avocado And Coconut Smoothie

Ingredients:

½ Cup Coconut Milk
½ Cup Coconut Water
½ cup 2 tbsp. Dutch-processed Cocoa
¼ cup Avocado
2 tbsp. Extra Virgin Coconut Oil
½ medium banana, sliced
-5 4Ice Cubes

Steps:
1.) Blend the leafy greens & liquids first at low speed for 1 min.
2.) Add the fruits & the rest of the ingredients. Blend at slow speed for 1 min.
3.) Move to medium speed until you see a vortex continue blending for 1 min.
4.) Blend at high speed for 1 min.

Chocolate Avocado And Dates Smoothie

Ingredients:
1 ¾ cup Coconut Water
3 pcs. dates
2 tbsp. Dutch-processed Cocoa
½ cup Avocado, pitted and sliced
¼ cup Figs

Steps:
1.) Blend the leafy greens & liquids first at low speed for 1 min.
2.) Add the fruits & the rest of the ingredients. Blend at slow speed for 1 min.
3.) Move to medium speed until you see a vortex continue blending for 1 min.
4.) Blend at high speed for 1 min.

Chocolate Avocado And Berry Smoothie

Ingredients:
1 cup Coconut Water

½ cup Avocado, pitted and sliced
2 tsp. Dutch-processed Cocoa
¼ cup Strawberries
¼ Cup Brewed Green Tea
4-5 Ice Cubes

Steps:
1.) Blend the leafy greens & liquids first at low speed for 1 min.
2.) Add the fruits & the rest of the ingredients. Blend at slow speed for 1 min.
3.) Move to medium speed until you see a vortex continue blending for 1 min.
4.) Blend at high speed for 1 min.

Chocolate Kiwi And Pineapple Smoothie

Ingredients:
1 Cup Coconut Water
1 tbsp. Dutch-processed Cocoa
½ Cup Kiwi, sliced
¼ Cup Pineapple, coarsely chopped
½ Cup Shredded Coconut

Steps:
1.) Blend the leafy greens & liquids first at low speed for 1 min.
2.) Add the fruits & the rest of the ingredients. Blend at slow speed for 1 min.
3.) Move to medium speed until you see a vortex continue blending for 1 min.
4.) Blend at high speed for 1 min.

Chapter 4: Chocolate Fruits and Greens Smoothies

Chocolaye Dates And Parsnip Smoothie

Ingredients:
1 Cup Unsweetened Almond Milk
2 Tbsp. Dutch-processed Cocoa
3 pcs. Dates
1/3 cup Instant Oats
1/3 Cup Parsnips
½ tsp. cinnamon
1 large banana

Steps:
1.) Blend the leafy greens & liquids first at low speed for 1 min.
2.) Add the fruits & the rest of the ingredients. Blend at slow speed for 1 min.
3.) Move to medium speed until you see a vortex continue blending for 1 min.
4.) Blend at high speed for 1 min.

Chocolate Avocado And Spinach Smoothie

Ingredients:
1 Cup Coconut Water
½ Tbsp. Dutch-processed Cocoa
¼ cup Avocado
¼ cup Spinach
1/4 cup Parsnips, peeled and coarsely chopped
5-6 Ice Cubes

Steps:
1.) Blend the leafy greens & liquids first at low speed for 1 min.
2.) Add the fruits & the rest of the ingredients. Blend at slow speed for 1 min.

3.) Move to medium speed until you see a vortex continue blending for 1 min.
4.) Blend at high speed for 1 min.

Chocolate Cherries And Mint Leaves Smoothie

Ingredients:
1 Cup Ice Cold Water
2 Tbsp. Dutch-processed Cocoa
¼ Cup Cherries
¼ Cup Mint Leaves Coarsely Chopped
½ tsp. Ground Coffee

Steps:
1.) Blend the leafy greens & liquids first at low speed for 1 min.
2.) Add the fruits & the rest of the ingredients. Blend at slow speed for 1 min.
3.) Move to medium speed until you see a vortex continue blending for 1 min.
4.) Blend at high speed for 1 min.

Chocolate Plums And Mint Leaves Smoothie

Ingredients:
1 Cup Dark Grape Juice
¼ Cup Almonds, Finely Ground
¼ Cup Plums, pitted
2 tsp. Dutch-processed Cocoa
¼ cup mint leaves coarsely chopped

Steps:
1.) Blend the leafy greens & liquids first at low speed for 1 min.
2.) Add the fruits & the rest of the ingredients. Blend at slow speed for 1 min.
3.) Move to medium speed until you see a vortex continue blending for 1 min.
4.) Blend at high speed for 1 min.

Chocolate Mango And Lettuce Smoothie

Ingredients:
1 Cup Coconut Water
½ cup Romaine Lettuce
1 Tbsp. Dutch-processed Cocoa
½ cup Mangoes, Pitted and Coarsely Sliced

Steps:
1.) Blend the leafy greens & liquids first at low speed for 1 min.
2.) Add the fruits & the rest of the ingredients. Blend at slow speed for 1 min.
3.) Move to medium speed until you see a vortex continue blending for 1 min.
4.) Blend at high speed for 1 min.

Chocolate Spinach And Grape Smoothie

Ingredients:
1 Cup Grape Juice
½ medium Cucumber
2 tbsp. Dutch-processed Cocoa
¼ cup Baby Spinach Leaves, coarsely chopped
¼ cup parsnips
4-5 Ice Cubes

Steps:
1.) Blend the leafy greens & liquids first at low speed for 1 min.
2.) Add the fruits & the rest of the ingredients. Blend at slow speed for 1 min.
3.) Move to medium speed until you see a vortex continue blending for 1 min.
4.) Blend at high speed for 1 min.

Chocolate Peanut Butter Kale And Date Smoothie

Ingredients:
1 Cup Unsweetened Almond Milk
2 tbsp. Peanut Butter

1 tbsp. Dutch-processed Cocoa Powder
½ cup Broccoli, coarsely chopped
3 pcs. Dates
½ cup Kale, coarsely chopped
4-5 Ice Cubes

Steps:
1.) Blend the leafy greens & liquids first at low speed for 1 min.
2.) Add the fruits & the rest of the ingredients. Blend at slow speed for 1 min.
3.) Move to medium speed until you see a vortex continue blending for 1 min.
4.) Blend at high speed for 1 min.

Chocolate Peaches Kale And Carrot Smoothie

Ingredients:
1 Cup Milk
2 tbsp. Dutch-processed Cocoa
¼ Cup Carrots, coarsely chopped
¼ Cup Kale, coarsely chopped
¼ cup Peaches, pitted and sliced
2 tbsp. Maple Syrup

Steps:
1.) Blend the leafy greens & liquids first at low speed for 1 min.
2.) Add the fruits & the rest of the ingredients. Blend at slow speed for 1 min.
3.) Move to medium speed until you see a vortex continue blending for 1 min.
4.) Blend at high speed for 1 min.

Chocolate Dandelion Greens And Nectarine Smoothie

Ingredients:
1 Cup Ice Cold Water

¼ Cup Blueberries
¼ Cup Nectarines
½ Tbsp. Dutch-processed Cocoa
½ Cup Dandelion Greens, coarsely chopped
Steps:
1.) Blend the leafy greens & liquids first at low speed for 1 min.
2.) Add the fruits & the rest of the ingredients. Blend at slow speed for 1 min.
3.) Move to medium speed until you see a vortex continue blending for 1 min.
4.) Blend at high speed for 1 min.

Chocolate Bell Pepper And Pear Smoothie
Ingredients:
1 Cup Unsweetened Almond Milk
¼ cup Pears, pitted
½ cup Green Bell Peppers, deseeded and frozen
4 ½ tsp. Dutch-processed Cocoa
4-5 Ice Cubes
Steps:
1.) Blend the leafy greens & liquids first at low speed for 1 min.
2.) Add the fruits & the rest of the ingredients. Blend at slow speed for 1 min.
3.) Move to medium speed until you see a vortex continue blending for 1 min.
4.) Blend at high speed for 1 min.

Chocolate Papaya And Bell Pepper Smoothie
Ingredients:
1 Cup Almond Milk
1 Tbsp. Dutch-processed Cocoa
¼ Cup Papaya, deseeded and coarsely chopped
¼ Cup Green Bell Peppers, deseeded and sliced

1 large banana, sliced

Steps:
1.) Blend the leafy greens & liquids first at low speed for 1 min.
2.) Add the fruits & the rest of the ingredients. Blend at slow speed for 1 min.
3.) Move to medium speed until you see a vortex continue blending for 1 min.
4.) Blend at high speed for 1 min.

Chocolate Dragon Fruit Spinach Green Tea Smoothie

Ingredients:
1 Cup Ice Cold Water
¼ cup Dragon Fruit, sliced
½ cup Baby Spinach Leaves, coarsely chopped
½ tbsp. Dutch-processed Cocoa
1 tsp. Match powder
5-6 Ice Cubes

Steps:
1.) Blend the leafy greens & liquids first at low speed for 1 min.
2.) Add the fruits & the rest of the ingredients. Blend at slow speed for 1 min.
3.) Move to medium speed until you see a vortex continue blending for 1 min.
4.) Blend at high speed for 1 min.

Chocolate Papaya Avocado And Kale Smoothie

Ingredients:
1 Cup Unsweetened Almond Milk
2 Tbsp. Dutch-processed Cocoa
¼ Cup Papaya, pitted and chopped
¼ Cup Avocado, pitted and chopped
¼ cup Kale leaves , coarsely chopped

5-6 Ice Cubes

Steps:
1.) Blend the leafy greens & liquids first at low speed for 1 min.
2.) Add the fruits & the rest of the ingredients. Blend at slow speed for 1 min.
3.) Move to medium speed until you see a vortex continue blending for 1 min.
4.) Blend at high speed for 1 min.

Chocolate Grape And Collard Greens Smoothie

Ingredients:
1 cup Ice Cold Water
¼ cup Collard Greens
¼ cup White Grapes
¼ tsp. cayenne pepper
¼ cup mint leaves, coarsely chopped
1 tbsp. Dutch-processed cocoa powder
1 large Banana, frozen

Steps:
1.) Blend the leafy greens & liquids first at low speed for 1 min.
2.) Add the fruits & the rest of the ingredients. Blend at slow speed for 1 min.
3.) Move to medium speed until you see a vortex continue blending for 1 min.
4.) Blend at high speed for 1 min.

Chocolate Red Cabbage And Dragon Fruit Smoothie

Ingredients:
1 cup Ice Cold Water
¼ cup pink Dragon Fruit

2 tsp. Dutch-processed Cocoa Powder
¼ cup Red Cabbage
¼ cup Beet Root
¼ cup Instant Oats

Steps:
1.) Blend the leafy greens & liquids first at low speed for 1 min.
2.) Add the fruits & the rest of the ingredients. Blend at slow speed for 1 min.
3.) Move to medium speed until you see a vortex continue blending for 1 min.
4.) Blend at high speed for 1 min.

Chocolate Cranberry And Lettuce Smoothie

Ingredients:
1 Cup Unsweetened Almond Milk
½ Cup Mangoes
¼ cup Dried Cranberries
¼ cup walnuts, finely chopped
½ tbsp. Dutch-processed Cocoa
¼ cup Romaine Lettuce
4-5 Ice Cubes

Steps:
1.) Blend the leafy greens & liquids first at low speed for 1 min.
2.) Add the fruits & the rest of the ingredients. Blend at slow speed for 1 min.
3.) Move to medium speed until you see a vortex continue blending for 1 min.
4.) Blend at high speed for 1 min.

Chocolate Dates And Lettuce Smoothie

Ingredients:
1 Cup Unsweetened Almond Milk
2 pcs. Dates, pitted
¼ Cup Pistachios finely ground

2 Tbsp. Dutch-processed Cocoa
¼ cup Romaine Lettuce, coarsely chopped
1 tbsp. Maple Syrup
4-5 Ice Cubes

Steps:
1.) Blend the leafy greens & liquids first at low speed for 1 min.
2.) Add the fruits & the rest of the ingredients. Blend at slow speed for 1 min.
3.) Move to medium speed until you see a vortex continue blending for 1 min.
4.) Blend at high speed for 1 min.

Chocolate Pear And Bell Pepper Smoothie

Ingredients:
1 ½ Cups Unsweetened Almond Milk
½ tsp. ground Ginger
½ cup Pear
½ tbsp. Dutch-processed Cocoa
¼ cup Green Bell Peppers, deseeded and Coarsely Chopped
4-5 Ice Cubes

Steps:
1.) Blend the leafy greens & liquids first at low speed for 1 min.
2.) Add the fruits & the rest of the ingredients. Blend at slow speed for 1 min.
3.) Move to medium speed until you see a vortex continue blending for 1 min.
4.) Blend at high speed for 1 min.

Chocolate Cherry And Triple Bell Pepper Smoothie

Ingredients:
1 cup Unsweetened Almond Milk
1 Cup Coconut Water
¼ cup cherries, pitted

¼ cup Red Bell Peppers, deseeded and coarsely chopped
½ cup Green Bell Peppers, deseeded and coarsely chopped
½ cup Yellow Bell Peppers, deseeded and coarsely chopped
½ tbsp. Dutch-processed Cocoa
¼ cup mint leaves coarsely chopped

Steps:
1.) Blend the leafy greens & liquids first at low speed for 1 min.
2.) Add the fruits & the rest of the ingredients. Blend at slow speed for 1 min.
3.) Move to medium speed until you see a vortex continue blending for 1 min.
4.) Blend at high speed for 1 min.

Chocolate Watermelon And Lettuce Smoothie

Ingredients:
1 Cup Coconut Milk
2 tbsp. Dutch-processed Cocoa
¼ Cup Romaine Lettuce
¼ cup Watermelon

Steps:
1.) Blend the leafy greens & liquids first at low speed for 1 min.
2.) Add the fruits & the rest of the ingredients. Blend at slow speed for 1 min.
3.) Move to medium speed until you see a vortex continue blending for 1 min.
4.) Blend at high speed for 1 min.

Chocolate Watermelon And Cucumber Smoothie

Ingredients:
1 Cup Unsweetened Almond Milk
¼ cup Watermelon, deseeded
½ medium Cucumber
1 Tbsp. Dutch-processed Cocoa

1 Large Banana
Steps:
1.) Blend the leafy greens & liquids first at low speed for 1 min.
2.) Add the fruits & the rest of the ingredients. Blend at slow speed for 1 min.
3.) Move to medium speed until you see a vortex continue blending for 1 min.
4.) Blend at high speed for 1 min.

Chapter 5: Meal Replacement Smoothies

Chocolate Coconut And Cucumber Smoothie

Ingredients:
1 Cup Almond Milk
¼ cup Shredded Coconut
2 tbsp. Dutch-processed Cocoa
½ medium cucumber
¼ cup Watermelon
1 large banana

Steps:
1.) Blend the leafy greens & liquids first at low speed for 1 min.
2.) Add the fruits & the rest of the ingredients. Blend at slow speed for 1 min.
3.) Move to medium speed until you see a vortex continue blending for 1 min.
4.) Blend at high speed for 1 min.

Chocolate Orange And Smoothie

Ingredients:
1 Cup Unsweetened Almond Milk
½ cup coconut milk
½ lemon, deseeded and coarsely chopped
2 tbsp. Dutch-processed Cocoa powder
½ cup Orange, deseeded and coarsely chopped
1 ounce melted chocolate
5-6 Ice Cubes

Steps:
1.) Blend the leafy greens & liquids first at low speed for 1 min.
2.) Add the fruits & the rest of the ingredients. Blend at slow speed for 1 min.

3.) Move to medium speed until you see a vortex continue blending for 1 min.
4.) Blend at high speed for 1 min.

Chocolate Apricots And Watermelon Protein Smoothie

Ingredients:
1 Cup Almond Milk
¼ Cup Grapes, deseeded
¼ Cup Apricots, coarsely chopped
¼ Cup Watermelon, deseeded and chopped
¼ cup, Canned Red Kidney Beans
2 tbsp. Dutch-processed cocoa powder
1 medium banana, sliced
Steps:
1.) Blend the leafy greens & liquids first at low speed for 1 min.
2.) Add the fruits & the rest of the ingredients. Blend at slow speed for 1 min.
3.) Move to medium speed until you see a vortex continue blending for 1 min.
4.) Blend at high speed for 1 min.

Chocolate Cucumber And Cabbage Smoothie

Ingredients:
1 Cup Unsweetened Almond Milk
2 Tbsp. Dutch-processed Cocoa
¼ Cup Cucumber, peeled and sliced
¼ Cup Watermelon, deseeded and coarsely chopped
¼ Cup Purple Cabbage, coarsely chopped
Steps:
1.) Blend the leafy greens & liquids first at low speed for 1 min.
2.) Add the fruits & the rest of the ingredients. Blend at slow speed for 1 min.

3.) Move to medium speed until you see a vortex continue blending for 1 min.
4.) Blend at high speed for 1 min.

Chocolate Lettuce And Raisins Protein Smoothie

Ingredients:
1 Cup Coconut Water
½ Cup Coconut Milk
2 tbsp. Dutch-processed Cocoa Powder
½ Cup Raisins, coarsely chopped
¼ Cup Romaine Lettuce, Coarsely Chopped
¼ cup Red Kidney Beans, rinsed and drained

Steps:
1.) Blend the leafy greens & liquids first at low speed for 1 min.
2.) Add the fruits & the rest of the ingredients. Blend at slow speed for 1 min.
3.) Move to medium speed until you see a vortex continue blending for 1 min.
4.) Blend at high speed for 1 min.

Chocolate Peanut Butter Protein Smoothie

Ingredients:
1 Cup Milk
½ cup Canned Red Kidney Beans, Drained and Rinsed
¼ Cup Tbsp. Dutch-processed Cocoa
2 tbsp. Peanut Butter
1 tbsp. Whey Protein Powder
4-5 Ice Cubes

Steps:
1.) Blend the leafy greens & liquids first at low speed for 1 min.
2.) Add the fruits & the rest of the ingredients. Blend at slow speed for 1 min.
3.) Move to medium speed until you see a vortex continue blending for 1 min.

4.) Blend at high speed for 1 min.

Chocolate Spinach And Coconut Smoothie

Ingredients:
½ Cup Coconut Milk
1 Cup Milk
½ large Banana, sliced
2 Tbsp. Dutch-processed Cocoa
2 oz. chocolate, melted
½ cup Baby Spinach Leaves Coarsely Chopped
4-5 Ice Cubes

Steps:
1.) Blend the leafy greens & liquids first at low speed for 1 min.
2.) Add the fruits & the rest of the ingredients. Blend at slow speed for 1 min.
3.) Move to medium speed until you see a vortex continue blending for 1 min.
4.) Blend at high speed for 1 min.

Chocolate Avocado And Double Green Protein Smoothie

Ingredients:
1 Cup Almond Milk
½ Cup Avocado
¼ Cup Romaine Lettuce
¼ Cup Baby Spinach Leaves, coarsely chopped
2 oz. chocolate, melted
1 tsp. Matcha powder
¼ cup canned red kidney beans, rinsed and drained

Steps:
1.) Blend the leafy greens & liquids first at low speed for 1 min.

2.) Add the fruits & the rest of the ingredients. Blend at slow speed for 1 min.
3.) Move to medium speed until you see a vortex continue blending for 1 min.
4.) Blend at high speed for 1 min.

Chocolate Peanut Butter And Lettuce Smoothie

Ingredients:
1 Cup Coconut Water
½ cup Almond Milk
¼ Cup Almonds, Finely Ground
2 Tbsp. Dutch-processed Cocoa
2 Tbsp. Peanut Butter
½ Cup Baby Spinach Leaves, coarsely chopped
¼ Cup Iceberg Lettuce

Steps:
1.) Blend the leafy greens & liquids first at low speed for 1 min.
2.) Add the fruits & the rest of the ingredients. Blend at slow speed for 1 min.
3.) Move to medium speed until you see a vortex continue blending for 1 min.
4.) Blend at high speed for 1 min.

Chocolate Pineapple And Mango Protein Smoothie

Ingredients:
1 Cup Coconut Milk
¼ cup Pineapple, sliced
¼ cup Mango, pitted and sliced
2 Tbsp. Dutch-processed Cocoa
½ Cup Canned Garbanzo Beans, rinsed and drained
4-5 Ice Cubes

Steps:
1.) Blend the leafy greens & liquids first at low speed for 1 min.

2.) Add the fruits & the rest of the ingredients. Blend at slow speed for 1 min.
3.) Move to medium speed until you see a vortex continue blending for 1 min.
4.) Blend at high speed for 1 min.

Chocolate Kale And Mango Protein Smoothie
Ingredients:
1 Cup Soya Milk
½ Tbsp. Dutch-processed Cocoa
½ Cup Canned Red Kidney Beans, Rinsed and Drained
¼ Cup Kale leaves, coarsely chopped
¼ Cup Mango, pitted and coarsely chopped
2 tbsp.
Steps:
1.) Blend the leafy greens & liquids first at low speed for 1 min.
2.) Add the fruits & the rest of the ingredients. Blend at slow speed for 1 min.
3.) Move to medium speed until you see a vortex continue blending for 1 min.
4.) Blend at high speed for 1 min.

Chocolate Orange And Mango Protein Lassi
Ingredients:
1 Cup Plain Yogurt
¼ Cup Mangoes, pitted and sliced
¼ Cup Orange, deseeded
2/3 Cup Canned Garbanzo Beans
½ Cup Dutch-processed Cocoa
5-6 Ice Cubes
Steps:
1.) Blend the leafy greens & liquids first at low speed for 1 min.

2.) Add the fruits & the rest of the ingredients. Blend at slow speed for 1 min.
3.) Move to medium speed until you see a vortex continue blending for 1 min.
4.) Blend at high speed for 1 min.

Chocolate Hazelnut Green Tea Protein Smoothie

Ingredients:
1 Cup Unsweetened Almond Milk
¼ Cup Hazelnuts finely ground
½ tsp. Matcha Powder
½ Cup Canned Red Kidney Beans, rinsed and drained
2 Tbsp. Dutch-processed Cocoa
5-6 Ice Cubes

Steps:
1.) Blend the leafy greens & liquids first at low speed for 1 min.
2.) Add the fruits & the rest of the ingredients. Blend at slow speed for 1 min.
3.) Move to medium speed until you see a vortex continue blending for 1 min.
4.) Blend at high speed for 1 min.

Chocolate Double Bean Green Tea Smoothie

Ingredients:
1 cup Milk
¼ cup Romaine Lettuce, coarsely chopped
¼ cup Spinach Leaves, coarsely chopped
¼ Cup Canned Red Kidney Beans, rinsed and drained
½ cup Canned Garbanzo Beans, rinsed and drained
 Tbsp. Dutch-processed Cocoa
1 Tbsp. Matcha Powder
1 large Banana, frozen

Steps:
1.) Blend the leafy greens & liquids first at low speed for 1 min.
2.) Add the fruits & the rest of the ingredients. Blend at slow speed for 1 min.
3.) Move to medium speed until you see a vortex continue blending for 1 min.
4.) Blend at high speed for 1 min.

Chocolate Coconut And Peaches Protein Smoothie

Ingredients:
1 cup Milk
¼ cup Peaches, pitted
¼ cup Canned White Beans, rinsed and drained
½ cup Shredded Coconut, coarsely chopped
¼ tsp. ground ginger
2 Tbsp. Dutch-processed Cocoa
½ cup Romaine Lettuce

Steps:
1.) Blend the leafy greens & liquids first at low speed for 1 min.
2.) Add the fruits & the rest of the ingredients. Blend at slow speed for 1 min.
3.) Move to medium speed until you see a vortex continue blending for 1 min.
4.) Blend at high speed for 1 min.

Chocolate Nectarine Protein Smoothie

Ingredients:
1 Cup Milk
2 Tbsp. Dutch-processed Cocoa
1/3 Cup White Kidney Beans, rinsed and drained
¼ cup Nectarines, pitted and sliced
¼ cup Baby Spinach Leaves, coarsely chopped
4-5 Ice Cubes

Steps:
1.) Blend the leafy greens & liquids first at low speed for 1 min.
2.) Add the fruits & the rest of the ingredients. Blend at slow speed for 1 min.
3.) Move to medium speed until you see a vortex continue blending for 1 min.
4.) Blend at high speed for 1 min.

Chocolate Apricot And Grapefruit Protein Smoothie

Ingredients:
1 Cup Grapefruit Juice
¼ cup Apricots
¼ Cup Canned White Kidney Beans, rinsed and drained
2 Tbsp. Dutch-processed Cocoa
¼ cup Baby Spinach Leaves, coarsely chopped
4-5 Ice Cubes

Steps:
1.) Blend the leafy greens & liquids first at low speed for 1 min.
2.) Add the fruits & the rest of the ingredients. Blend at slow speed for 1 min.
3.) Move to medium speed until you see a vortex continue blending for 1 min.
4.) Blend at high speed for 1 min.

Chocolate Bell Pepper Protein Smoothie

Ingredients:
1 Cup Unsweetened Almond Milk
½ tsp. ground Ginger
½ cup Yellow Bell Pepper, pitted
¼ Cup Canned Red Kidney Beans, , rinsed and drained
1 Tbsp. Dutch-processed Cocoa
½ large banana
4-5 Ice Cubes

Steps:
1.) Blend the leafy greens & liquids first at low speed for 1 min.
2.) Add the fruits & the rest of the ingredients. Blend at slow speed for 1 min.
3.) Move to medium speed until you see a vortex continue blending for 1 min.
4.) Blend at high speed for 1 min.

Chocolate Citrus And Protein Lassi

Ingredients:
1 cup Plain Yogurt
¼ Cup Canned Garbanzo Beans, rinsed and drained
2 Tbsp. Dutch-processed Cocoa
½ cup Orange, deseeded and coarsely chopped
½ cup Lemon, deseeded and coarsely chopped
¼ cup Parsnips, peeled and coarsely chopped, chopped

Steps:
1.) Blend the leafy greens & liquids first at low speed for 1 min.
2.) Add the fruits & the rest of the ingredients. Blend at slow speed for 1 min.
3.) Move to medium speed until you see a vortex continue blending for 1 min.
4.) Blend at high speed for 1 min.

Chocolate Kale And Protein Smoothie

Ingredients:
1 Cup Coconut Milk
½ Cup Canned Garbanzo Beans, rinsed and drained
½ Cup Grapefruit, deseeded and coarsely chopped
¼ Cup Tbsp. Dutch-processed Cocoa
¼ Cup Kale, stems removed and coarsely chopped

Steps:
1.) Blend the leafy greens & liquids first at low speed for 1 min.
2.) Add the fruits & the rest of the ingredients. Blend at slow speed for 1 min.
3.) Move to medium speed until you see a vortex continue blending for 1 min.
4.) Blend at high speed for 1 min.

Chocolate Peanut Butter And Apple Protein Lassi

Ingredients:
1 cup Plain Yogurt

¼ cup Apples, deseeded and coarsely chopped
¼ cup Red Kidney Beans, rinsed and drained
2 tbsp. Peanut Butter
½ tsp. Cinnamon
½ tsp. Nutmeg
2 Tbsp. Dutch-processed Cocoa
1 large Banana

Steps:
1.) Blend the leafy greens & liquids first at low speed for 1 min.
2.) Add the fruits & the rest of the ingredients. Blend at slow speed for 1 min.
3.) Move to medium speed until you see a vortex continue blending for 1 min.
4.) Blend at high speed for 1 min.

Chapter 6: Cheat Day Smoothies

Chocolate Grape Smoothie

Ingredients:
1 Cup Unsweetened Almond Milk
½ Cup Grape Juice
¼ Cup Grapes, frozen
2 oz. melted chocolate
1 tsp. Dutch-processed cocoa powder
2-3 tsp. sugar (optional)
½ medium Banana, sliced

Steps:
1.) Blend the leafy greens & liquids first at low speed for 1 min.
2.) Add the fruits & the rest of the ingredients. Blend at slow speed for 1 min.
3.) Move to medium speed until you see a vortex continue blending for 1 min.
4.) Blend at high speed for 1 min.

Chocolate Peanut Butter And Hazelnut Smoothie

Ingredients:
1 Cup Coconut Milk
2 Oz. bittersweet chocolate, melted
1 med. Banana, sliced
2 tbsp. Peanut Butter
¼ Cup Hazelnut, finely ground
2-3 tsp. sugar(optional)
5-6 Ice Cubes

Steps:
1.) Blend the leafy greens & liquids first at low speed for 1 min.

2.) Add the fruits & the rest of the ingredients. Blend at slow speed for 1 min.
3.) Move to medium speed until you see a vortex continue blending for 1 min.
4.) Blend at high speed for 1 min.

Chocolate Mint Smoothie

Ingredients:
1 Cup Milk
½ Cup Cherries, pitted
¼ Cup Mint leaves, coarsely chopped
2 Oz. bittersweet chocolate, melted
2-3 tsp. sugar(optional)
Steps:
1.) Blend the leafy greens & liquids first at low speed for 1 min.
2.) Add the fruits & the rest of the ingredients. Blend at slow speed for 1 min.
3.) Move to medium speed until you see a vortex continue blending for 1 min.
4.) Blend at high speed for 1 min.

Chocolate Pecan And Macadamia Smoothie

Ingredients:
1 Cup Unsweetened Almond Milk
2 Oz. bittersweet chocolate, melted
¼ Cup Pecans, finely ground
¼ Cup Oats
1 medium Banana, sliced
1 tbsp. macadamia nut oil
1 tbsp. sugar (optional)
Steps:
1.) Blend the leafy greens & liquids first at low speed for 1 min.
2.) Add the fruits & the rest of the ingredients. Blend at slow speed for 1 min.

3.) Move to medium speed until you see a vortex continue blending for 1 min.

4.) Blend at high speed for 1 min.

Double Chocolate And Peanut Butter Smoothie

Ingredients:

1 Cup Coconut Milk

¼ cup Beet Root

1 tsp. Dutch-processed Cocoa Powder

2 tbsp. Peanut Butter

2 Oz. bittersweet chocolate, melted

2-3 tsp. sugar(optional)

Steps:

1.) Blend the leafy greens & liquids first at low speed for 1 min.

2.) Add the fruits & the rest of the ingredients. Blend at slow speed for 1 min.

3.) Move to medium speed until you see a vortex continue blending for 1 min.

4.) Blend at high speed for 1 min.

Chocolate Blueberry Smoothie

Ingredients:

1 cup coconut milk

2 Oz. bittersweet chocolate, melted

¾ cup Blueberries

1 tbsp. sugar

4-5 Ice Cubes

Steps:

1.) Blend the leafy greens & liquids first at low speed for 1 min.

2.) Add the fruits & the rest of the ingredients. Blend at slow speed for 1 min.

3.) Move to medium speed until you see a vortex continue blending for 1 min.

4.) Blend at high speed for 1 min.

Chocolate Peach And Mango Smoothie

Ingredients:
1 Cup Coconut Water
¼ Cup Oz. bittersweet chocolate, melted
¼ Cup Peaches, pitted and sliced
¼ cup Mangoes, pitted and sliced
½ large banana
2-3 tsp. sugar(optional)
4-5 Ice Cubes

Steps:
1.) Blend the leafy greens & liquids first at low speed for 1 min.
2.) Add the fruits & the rest of the ingredients. Blend at slow speed for 1 min.
3.) Move to medium speed until you see a vortex continue blending for 1 min.
4.) Blend at high speed for 1 min.

Chocolate Peaches And Date Smoothie

Ingredients:
2 Cups Coconut Water
½ Cup Peaches, pitted and sliced
2-3 pcs. Dates
1 Ounce. bittersweet chocolate, melted
¼ cup Mint Leaves, coarsely chopped
2-3 tsp. maple syrup(optional)

Steps:
1.) Blend the leafy greens & liquids first at low speed for 1 min.
2.) Add the fruits & the rest of the ingredients. Blend at slow speed for 1 min.
3.) Move to medium speed until you see a vortex continue blending for 1 min.
4.) Blend at high speed for 1 min.

Chocolate Pineapple And Kiwi Smoothie

Ingredients:

½ Cup Milk
½ Cup Coconut Milk
¼ Cup Kiwi, sliced
1 ounce bittersweet chocolate, melted
½ Cup Pineapple, sliced
¼ cup Shredded Coconut
5-6 Ice Cubes
2-3 tsp. muscovado sugar (optional)

Steps:
1.) Blend the leafy greens & liquids first at low speed for 1 min.
2.) Add the fruits & the rest of the ingredients. Blend at slow speed for 1 min.
3.) Move to medium speed until you see a vortex continue blending for 1 min.
4.) Blend at high speed for 1 min.

Chocolate Avocado And Mango Smoothie

Ingredients:
1 Cup Milk
¼ cup Avocado, pitted and sliced
¼ cup Mango, pitted and sliced
1 ounce bittersweet chocolate, melted
2-3 tsp. sugar (optional)
4-5 Ice Cubes

Steps:
1.) Blend the leafy greens & liquids first at low speed for 1 min.
2.) Add the fruits & the rest of the ingredients. Blend at slow speed for 1 min.
3.) Move to medium speed until you see a vortex continue blending for 1 min.
4.) Blend at high speed for 1 min.

Chocolate Nutella And Peanut Butter Smoothie

Ingredients:
1 Cup Unsweetened Almond Milk

1 ounce bittersweet chocolate, melted
½ tsp Ginger
½ tsp. Cinnamon
½ tsp. Nutmeg
1 tbsp. Nutella
1 tbsp. Peanut Butter
½ Cup Cherries

Steps:
1.) Blend the leafy greens & liquids first at low speed for 1 min.
2.) Add the fruits & the rest of the ingredients. Blend at slow speed for 1 min.
3.) Move to medium speed until you see a vortex continue blending for 1 min.
4.) Blend at high speed for 1 min.

Chocolate Red Bean Smoothie

Ingredients:
1 Cup Unsweetened Almond Milk
¼ Cup canned Red Beans, rinsed and drained
½ cup hazelnuts, finely Ground
1 Ounce bittersweet chocolate, melted
2-3 tsp. sugar (optional)
5-6 Ice Cubes

Steps:
1.) Blend the leafy greens & liquids first at low speed for 1 min.
2.) Add the fruits & the rest of the ingredients. Blend at slow speed for 1 min.
3.) Move to medium speed until you see a vortex continue blending for 1 min.
4.) Blend at high speed for 1 min.

White Chocolate Macadamia And Cherry Smoothie

Ingredients:
1 Cup Unsweetened Milk

½ Cup Macadamia Nuts, finely ground
¼ Cup Cherries, pitted
2 Oz. white chocolate, melted
2-3 tsp. sugar (optional)
1 tbsp. macadamia nut oil
5-6 Ice Cubes

Steps:
1.) Blend the leafy greens & liquids first at low speed for 1 min.
2.) Add the fruits & the rest of the ingredients. Blend at slow speed for 1 min.
3.) Move to medium speed until you see a vortex continue blending for 1 min.
4.) Blend at high speed for 1 min.

White Chocolate Green Tea Smoothie
Ingredients:
1 cup Milk
½ Cup Strawberries
1 ounce White Chocolate
1 ounce bittersweet chocolate, melted
2 tsp. Matcha Green Tea
1 tbsp. Macadamia Nut Oil

Steps:
1.) Blend the leafy greens & liquids first at low speed for 1 min.
2.) Add the fruits & the rest of the ingredients. Blend at slow speed for 1 min.
3.) Move to medium speed until you see a vortex continue blending for 1 min.
4.) Blend at high speed for 1 min.

Chocolate Purple Smoothie
Ingredients:
1 cup Dark Grape Juice
¼ cup dark grapes, deseeded

¼ cup Blueberries
½ cup Plums, pitted
2 Oz. bittersweet chocolate, melted
2-3 tsp. sugar(optional)
Steps:
1.) Blend the leafy greens & liquids first at low speed for 1 min.
2.) Add the fruits & the rest of the ingredients. Blend at slow speed for 1 min.
3.) Move to medium speed until you see a vortex continue blending for 1 min.
4.) Blend at high speed for 1 min.

Chocolate Almonds And Peaches Smoothie

Ingredients:
1 Cup Unsweetened Almond Milk
2 Oz. bittersweet chocolate, melted
1/3 cup peaches, pitted
¼ cup Apples, deseeded and coarsely chopped
2-3 tsp. sugar (optional)
4-5 Ice Cubes
Steps:
1.) Blend the leafy greens & liquids first at low speed for 1 min.
2.) Add the fruits & the rest of the ingredients. Blend at slow speed for 1 min.
3.) Move to medium speed until you see a vortex continue blending for 1 min.
4.) Blend at high speed for 1 min.

Chocolate Cookie Butter Smoothie

Ingredients:
1 Cup Ice Cold Water
1 tbsp. Cookie Butter
1 tbsp. Peanut Butter
1 ounce bittersweet chocolate, melted
¼ cup Plums, pitted

1 large Banana, sliced
2-3 tsp. sugar(optional)
4-5 Ice Cubes

Steps:
1.) Blend the leafy greens & liquids first at low speed for 1 min.
2.) Add the fruits & the rest of the ingredients. Blend at slow speed for 1 min.
3.) Move to medium speed until you see a vortex continue blending for 1 min.
4.) Blend at high speed for 1 min.

Chocolate Avocado And Macadamia Green Tea Smoothie

Ingredients:
1 Cup Almond Milk
½ cup Brewed Green Tea
½ tsp. Macadamia Nut Oil
¼ Cup Oz. bittersweet chocolate, melted
¼ cup Avocado, pitted and sliced
2-3 tsp. sugar(optional)
4-5 Ice Cubes

Steps:
1.) Blend the leafy greens & liquids first at low speed for 1 min.
2.) Add the fruits & the rest of the ingredients. Blend at slow speed for 1 min.
3.) Move to medium speed until you see a vortex continue blending for 1 min.
4.) Blend at high speed for 1 min.

Chocolate Coconut And Tropical Fruit Smoothie

Ingredients:
1 cup Ice Cold Water
1 ounce bittersweet chocolate, melted
¼ cup Mangoes, pitted
¼ cup Pineapple, sliced

¼ cup Shredded Coconut
½ tsp mint extract
2-3 tsp. sugar(optional)
Steps:
1.) Blend the leafy greens & liquids first at low speed for 1 min.
2.) Add the fruits & the rest of the ingredients. Blend at slow speed for 1 min.
3.) Move to medium speed until you see a vortex continue blending for 1 min.
4.) Blend at high speed for 1 min.

White Chocolate Raisin Smoothie

Ingredients:
1 Cup Milk
1 ounce white chocolate
1 ounce bittersweet chocolate, melted
¼ cup Raisins
2-3 tsp. sugar(optional)
Steps:
1.) Blend the leafy greens & liquids first at low speed for 1 min.
2.) Add the fruits & the rest of the ingredients. Blend at slow speed for 1 min.
3.) Move to medium speed until you see a vortex continue blending for 1 min.
4.) Blend at high speed for 1 min.

Chocolate Avocado And Nectarine Smoothie

Ingredients:
1 Cup Milk
½ Cup Coconut Milk
½ Cup Nectarine
¼ cup Shredded Coconut
1 cup Avocadoes
1 Ounce bittersweet chocolate, melted

¼ cup Mangoes
2-3 tsp. sugar(optional)
Steps:
1.) Blend the leafy greens & liquids first at low speed for 1 min.
2.) Add the fruits & the rest of the ingredients. Blend at slow speed for 1 min.
3.) Move to medium speed until you see a vortex continue blending for 1 min.
4.) Blend at high speed for 1 min.

Dark Chocolate & Sea Salt Cookies

This recipe makes 24 servings
1-1/4 cups Gold Medal all-purpose-flour
1/3 cup unsweetened cocoa-powder
1/2 tsp. baking-soda
3/4 cup butter, softened
1/2 cup Truvia Baking Blend
2 tsps. vanilla
1 egg
1/2 cup mini semi-sweet-chocolate-chips
1 tblsp Truvia Baking Blends
3 tblsps water
1 tsp. coarse sea salt
TIME TO PREP
15 mins
COOK
15 mins
READY TO SERVE IN
39 mins
Directions
Heat the oven - 325 Deg. F.
In medium bowl, mix flour, cocoa and baking-soda; set aside.

In large bowl, beat butter, 1/2 cup Truvia Baking-Blend, vanilla & egg on medium speed using your with elec. mixer, or mix with spoon.
Stir in flour mixture. Stir in chocolate-chips.
Drop dough by rounded tblsps on ungreased cookie sheet.
Press down on them slightly.
Bake 13 - 15 mins. or just until set. Cool 1 to 2 mins.; remove from cookie sheet over to a cooling rack for final cooling (about 15 mins).
Meanwhile, in a small bowl, beat in1 tblsp Truvia Baking-Blend with water.
Brush it over cookies (discard any of the remaining water mix); sprinkle with sea salt.

Caramel Pecan Cinnamon Roll Cookies

This recipe makes 36 servings
2 1/4 cups bread flour
1 tblsp ground style cinnamon
1 tsp. salt
1 tsp. baking-soda
1-1/4 cups brown sugar
1 cup butter, melted
1/4 cup white sugar
1 egg
1 egg yolk
2 tblsps milk
1-1/2 tsps. vanilla ext.
1 cup white chocolate-chips
1 cup pecan pieces
12 individually wrapped caramels, unwrapped, or more as needed
TIME TO PREP
15 mins
COOK
15 mins

READY TO SERVE IN
1 hr

Directions

Whisk flour, cinnamon, salt, and baking-soda together in a bowl. brown sugar, butter, and white sugar together in a separate bowl; add egg, egg yolk, milk, and vanilla ext.; stir until well mixed.

Slowly stir flour mixture in to butter-sugar mixture until dough is thoroughly combined; fold in white chocolate-chips and pecans.

Refrigerate dough until chilled, at least 30 mins.

Pre-heat oven to 375 Deg. F (190 Deg. C).

Scoop dough by rounded tblsps on to a baking sheet.

Bake in the pre-heated oven for 7 mins.; rotate baking sheet and continue baking until cookies are golden brown, about 8 mins. more.

Transfer cookies to a wire rack to cool completely.

Place caramels in a microwave-safe bowl; heat in microwave until melted, 30 seconds to 1 minute.

Drizzle melted caramel over cooled cookies.

Ghirardelli Black & Whites

This recipe makes apx. 45 cookies
2 large egg-whites
1/2 tsp. vanilla ext.
1/8 tsp. cream of tartar
1/2 cup granulated sugar
1-1/2 cups Ghirardelli brand (60% Cacao) Bitter-sweet Chocolate Baking Chips
2/3 cup whipping cream
1/2 tsp. vanilla ext.
1/4 cup fine chopped pistachios (this is optional)
TIME TO PREP
30 mins
COOK
10 mins

READY TO SERVE IN
40 mins

Directions

Place egg whites in a med sized bowl; let it stand at room temp. for 30 mins.

Pre-heat oven to 325 Deg. F. Line 2 large sheets with foil &set aside.

Add the 1/2 tsp. vanilla and the 1/8 tsp. cream of tartar to the egg whites.

Beat with a mixer set at medium until gentle peaks appear (the tips will curl).

Add sugar 1 tblsp at a time – now beating on high until stiffer peaks start to form (tips will stand up straight).

Drop in the egg white mix by even sized tsps. Placed 1-1/2 inches apart on prepped baking sheets.

Use the back side of the spoon. To place a small dent in the middle of each cookie.

Bake both sheets on a separate rack level for 10 mins. Turn oven off & let cookies dry in the sealed oven for about 40 mins.

Transfer warm cookies to bake racks to let cool.*

For filling,

Using a micro-wave-safe bowl, blend Ghirardelli® Chips, whipcream and the 1/4 tsp. vanilla.

Heat on medium setting (50 percent) for 1 min., stirring mix every 30 secs or so.

Remove & final stir. If chocolate is'nt melted enough, return and repeat for another 15 to 20 secs.

However, always be careful to avoid scorching! Stir melted mix until it becomes smooth.

Let cool slightly and spoon thefilling in to cooled meringues.

** If desired you can sprinkle with pistachios too!

Enjoy right away.

Chocolate Chipped Granola Cookies

This recipe makes 3 1/2 dozen cookies

Crisco® No-Stick cook spray
1/2 cup Crisco® Bakers Sticks (or equivalent all vegetable type shortening)
1 cup firmly packed brown-sugar
2 large eggs
2 tblsps milk
2 tsps. vanilla ext.
1 3/4 cups All Purpose Flour
3/4 tsp. salt
1/2 tsp. baking-soda
2 1/2 cups pkgd granola
1 cup semi-sweet chocolate-chips

Directions
Heat oven up to 350 Deg. F.
Coat your baking sheets with a non-stick cooking spray.
Beat together shortening & brown sugar in a large bowl with a mixer set on med. until creamy.
Beat in 2 eggs, vanilla and milk.
Combine flour, baking-soda and salt in medium bowl.
Add 2 eggs to the mixture.
Bled well and stir in granola along with the chocolate-chips.
Distribute by even tblspfuls on to a prepped baking sheet.
Bake 9 - 10 mins. or until bottoms begin to get slightly browned.
Let cool for2 mins.
Remove away to wire bake rack to cool completely.

Cinnamon & White Chocolate Cookies

This recipe makes 2 dozen cookies
1/2 cup butter, softened
1/2 cup shortening
3/4 cup white sugar
1/2 cup packed brown-sugar
1 egg
2 tsps. vanilla ext.
1 3/4 cups all-purpose-flour

1 tsp. baking-soda
1/2 tsp. salt
10 ounces white chocolate (chopped)
1/2 tsp. ground-style cinnamon
TIME TO PREP
15 mins
COOK
15 mins
READY TO SERVE IN
2 hrs

Directions

Beat together butter with shortening until creamy & smooth then gradually add in white sugar & brown sugars, beating everything at med speed until fully incorporated.
Beat in 1 egg with vanilla ext.
Combine flour, salt & baking-soda in another bowl
Blend in with butter mixture until fully incorporated.
Fold in white chocolate & cinnamon.
Refrigerate the resulting dough for an hour.
Pre-heat the oven at 350 Deg. F. (175 Deg. C). and lightly grease 2 baking sheets.
Lay out the dough by the large tblspful on to your prepped baking sheets, leave about 3 inches between each cookie.
Bake until cookies are slightly brown around the edges, 12 - 14 mins.
Let stand on the sheets for 10 mins. Then move to cool completely on a wire bake rack until they become firm.

Chocolate Chip Cookies 1.0

This recipe makes 1 dozen
1/2 cup shortening
1/4 cup white sugar
1/2 cup packed brown sugar
1 egg
1/2 tsp. vanilla ext.

1 1/8 cups all-purpose-flour
1/2 tsp. baking-soda
1/2 tsp. salt
1/2 cup chopped walnuts
1 cup semi-sweet chocolate-chips
TIME TO PREP
15 mins
COOK
8 mins
READY TO SERVE IN
23 mins

Directions

Pre-heat oven to 350 Deg. F. (175 Deg. C).

In a medium volume bowl, cream together shortening, brown & white sugar.

Mix in the egg and vanilla. Combine the flour, baking-soda and salt; stir in to the batter until moistened.

Mix in the walnuts and chocolate-chips. Drop by heaping spoonfuls on to an ungreased cookie-sheet..

Bake for apx. 8 mins in the pre-heated oven, until the edges are light-brown.

Grandma's Choco-Chip Delights

This recipe makes 6 dozen
4 1/2 cups all-purpose-flour
2 tsps. baking-soda
2 tsps. salt
2 cups butter, softened
1-1/2 cups white sugar
1-1/2 cups packed brown sugar
2 tsps. vanilla ext.
4 eggs
8 cups semi-sweet chocolate-chips
3 cups chopped walnuts
2 cups candy-coated milk-chocolate pieces

Directions

Pre-heat oven to 375 Deg. F (190 Deg. C).
Mix flour, baking-soda and salt In a small volume bowl.
Beat butter, sugars and vanilla in a huge bowl.
Beat eggs WELL and add to flour mixture.
Mix flour mixture in to butter mixture and stir well.
Add the semi-sweet chocolate pieces and walnuts. Mix well.
Distribute by rounded tblsps on ungreased baking sheets. (I lightly push about 4-6 plain M and M's on top of each cookie for flavor and color.)
Bake for 11 mins. Don't overbake or they get hard. Let cool on wire cooling racks. Enjoy!

Banana-Apple Chocolate Chunk Cookies

This recipe makes 18 cookies
1 very ripe banana
1/2 cup applesauce
1/2 cup honey
1/3 cup almond butter
1/4 cup butter
1 egg
2/3 cup coconut flour
1/2 cup oats
1/2 cup dark chocolate-chunks
1/3 cup tapioca flour
1 tsp. baking-soda
1/2 tsp. ground style cinnamon
1 dash of salt
TIME TO PREP
15 mins
COOK
15 mins
READY TO SERVE IN
1 hr

Directions

Pre-heat oven to 350 Deg. F. (175 Deg. C).

Mash banana, applesauce, and honey together in a bowl; add almond butter, butter, egg and stir until combined.

Add coconut flour, oats, chocolate-chunks, tapioca flour, baking-soda, cinnamon, and salt to banana mixture, stir until dry ingredients are moist and form a dough.

Drop rounded tblspfuls of dough on to Prepped baking sheet.

Bake until slightly brown, about 15 mins. Let cool to room temperature, about 30 mins.

Freckles 'N Bumps

This recipe makes 3 dozen
1/2 cup butter, softened
1 1/8 cups packed brown sugar
1/2 cup applesauce
2 eggs
1 tsp. vanilla ext.
3 1/2 cups all-purpose-flour
1-1/2 tsps. baking-soda
1/2 tsp. salt
1-1/4 cups semi-sweet chocolate-chips
1-1/4 cups white chocolate-chips
4 cups shelled walnuts
TIME TO PREP
15 mins
COOK
10 mins
READY TO SERVE IN
45 mins

Directions

Pre-heat your oven to 375 Deg. F (190 Deg. C). Grease your cookie sheets.

In a large volume bowl, stir together the butter, brown sugar, applesauce, eggs & vanilla.

Combine the flour, baking-soda and salt, gradually stir in to the applesauce mixture.

Fold in the chocolate-chips, white chocolate-chips and walnuts until evenly distributed.

Distribute by rounded spoonfuls on to the prepared cookie sheets.

Bake for 8 - 10 mins. in the pre-heated oven. Allow the hot cookies to cool down on your baking sheet for 5 mins. before moving over to a wire rack to finish cooling down completely.

Passover Chocolate-Chip Cookies

This recipe makes 5-dozen
3/4 cup chopped walnuts (optional)
1 cup matzo cake-meal
1/4 tsp. salt
1/2 cup potato-starch
3 eggs
1/2 cup margarine (softened)
1-1/4 cups white sugar
1 (12 ounce) bag chocolate-chips
TIME TO PREP
15 mins
COOK
10 mins
READY TO SERVE IN
25 mins

Directions

Pre-heat oven to 275 Deg. F (135 Deg. C).

Spread out walnuts on to a bake sheet, then toast until the nuts turn golden brown & fragrant, (about 45 mins).

Monitor nuts often as they bake because they can burn quickly. Once they are toasted, set them aside to cool to room temp.

Increase oven temp.to 350 Deg. F. (175 Deg. C). and line your baking sheets with a parchment paper.

Whisk the matzo-cake-meal, salt, and potato starch together in a big bowl.

In another large volume bowl, beat 3 eggs, margarine &sugar together until smooth.

Stir the meal mix in to the wet slurry until thoroughly combined & mix in the chocolate-chips.

Drop in the dough by spoonfuls on to the parchment-lined baking sheets.
Bake in the pre-heated oven until light golden brown, 10 - 15 mins.
Remove cookies from the bake sheets as soon as they are taken from the oven; set out to cool on racks.

Minnesota's Favorite Cookie

This recipe makes 4 dozen
1 cup butter, softened
1-1/2 cups brown sugar
2 eggs
2 tsps. vanilla ext.
2 1/2 cups all-purpose-flour
1 tsp. baking-powder
1/4 tsp. salt
1 cup milk-chocolate-chips
1/2 cup semi-sweet chocolate-chips
2/3 cup toffee baking bits
1 cup chopped pecans
TIME TO PREP
15 mins
COOK
10 mins
READY TO SERVE IN
25 mins

Directions
Pre-heat oven to 350 Deg. F. (175 Deg. C). Grease your cookie sheets.
In a medium volume bowl, cream together the butter & sugar.
Beat in 2 eggs, one-by-one, then stir in the vanilla.
Combine the flour, baking-powder, and salt; stir it all in to the creamed mix.
Stir in the milk-chocolate and semi-sweet chips, toffee bits, and pecans.

Drop by tblspfuls on to cookie sheets.
Bake for around 10 - 12 mins. in your pre-heated oven.
Allow cookies to sit and cool on the baking sheet before transferring to wire cooling racks to cool completely.

Kitchen-Sink Cookies

This recipe makes 5 dozen
1 cup butter, softened
2 cups packed brown sugar
2 eggs
2 tsps. vanilla ext.
2 1/3 cups all-purpose-flour
1 tsp. baking-soda
1 tsp. salt
2 cups rolled oats
1 cup semi-sweet chocolate-chips
1 cup vanilla baking chips
1/2 cup butterscotch chips
1 cup chopped pecans
TIME TO PREP
15 mins
COOK
12 mins
READY TO SERVE IN
30 mins

Directions
Pre-heat your oven to 375 Deg. F (190 Deg. C).
In a larger volume bowl, cream together 1 cup of butter & brown sugar until smooth.
Beat 2 eggs in to the mix one-by-one then add in vanilla.
Combine the flour, baking-soda and salt; stir it all in to the creamed mix.
Mix in the oats, chocolate-chips, vanilla chips, butterscotch chips and chopped pecans.
Deposit on ungreased baking sheets in tblspn sized portions.

Cookies should be at least 2 inches apart.
Bake for 8 - 10 mins. in the pre-heated oven.
Allow the hot cookies to cool down on your baking sheet for 5 mins. before moving over to a wire rack to finish cooling down completely.

Double Chocolate Mint Cookies

This recipe makes 6 - 8 dozen
2 1/2 cups butter, softened
4 cups white sugar
4 eggs
1 tsp. vanilla ext.
1 tsp. peppermint ext.
4 cups all-purpose-flour
1-1/2 cups un-sweetened cocoa-powder
2 tsps. baking-soda
1 tsp. salt
2 cups semi-sweet chocolate-chips
TIME TO PREP
25 mins
COOK
8 mins
READY TO SERVE IN
33 mins

Directions

Pre-heat oven to 350 Deg. F. (175 Deg. C).
Cream together, 2 ½ cups of softened butter, sugar and 4 eggs.
Mix in rest of the ingredients & blend everything fully.
Drop by tsp.ful on to a cookie sheet.
Bake at 350 Deg. F. (175 Deg. C) for 8-9 mins.
Cookies should be soft at this point.
Let cool for about a minute then remove to a wire rack to cool completely.

Almond Chocolate & Coconut Cookies

This recipe makes 4 dozen
1 cup butter
1-1/2 cups white sugar
1-1/2 cups brown sugar
4 eggs
4 tsps. vanilla ext.
4 1/2 cups all-purpose-flour
2 tsps. baking-soda
1 tsp. salt
5 cups semi-sweet chocolate-chips
2 cups flaked coconut
2 cups chopped almonds
TIME TO PREP
10 mins
COOK
13 mins
READY TO SERVE IN
25 mins

Directions

Pre-heat your oven to 375 Deg. F (190 Deg. C). Grease your cookie sheets.
In a large volume bowl, cream together the white sugar, butter and brown sugar until smooth.
Beat in the eggs, one-by-one, then stir in the vanilla.
Combine the flour, baking-soda and salt, stir it all in to the creamed mix until completely blended.
Lasty, stir in 5 cups of chocolate-chips, coconut & almonds.
Lay out by rounded spoonfuls on to the prepped cookie sheets.
Bake for 8 - 10 mins. in the oven then allow the cookies to cool down for a few minutes on your baking sheet before moving over to a wire rack to finish cooling down completely.

Lodge Cookies

This recipe makes 5 dozen cookies

2 cups butter
2 cups white sugar
2 cups packed brown sugar
4 eggs
2 tsps. vanilla ext.
3 cups all-purpose-flour
2 tsps. salt
2 tsps. baking-soda
6 cups quick cooking oats
2 cups chocolate-chips
2 cups chopped & toasted-walnuts
1 cup coconut
1 cup raisins
TIME TO PREP
20 mins
COOK
12 mins
READY TO SERVE IN
32 mins

Directions

Pre-heat your oven to 350 Deg. F. (175 Deg. C).
Grease your cookie sheets.
In a very large bowl, cream together the butter, brown & white sugar until smooth.
Beat in 4 eggs to the mix one-by-one then add 2 tspns of vanilla.
Combine the flour, salt & baking-soda; stir in to the sugar being sure to mix until everything is well incorporated.
Next, mix in oats, then stir in the chocolate-chips, nuts, raisins and coconut.
Drop by heaping tsp.fuls on to the prepped cookie sheets.
Bake for around 10 - 12 mins. in your pre-heated oven, or until golden brown.
Let cookies cool for a few mins. on the cookie sheets before removing to wire racks to cool completely.

Chocolate Doodles

This recipe makes 6 dozen
1/2 cup vegetable oil
4 (1 ounce) squares unsweetened chocolate, melted
2 cups white sugar
1 cup egg substitute
2 tsps. vanilla ext.
1/4 tsp. salt
2 tsps. baking-powder
2 cups all-purpose-flour
1 cup confectioners' sugar

Directions

Mix the oil, melted 1 oz of chocolate, & sugar in a large glass mixing bowl.
Blend in 1 cup of egg substitute or you may use egg whites if no other solution exists.
Blend with vanilla. Stir in salt, baking-powder & flour in to the oil mix.
Chill overnight.
Drop tsp.fuls of dough in to confectioners sugar.
Roll through the sugar then shape result in to balls.
Space out 2 inches apart on pre-greased cookie sheet.
Flatten with bottom of a glass pre-dipped in the confectioners sugar.
Bake 10 - 12 mins. at 350 Deg. F. (175 Deg. C).
Do not let over-bake.

Scooter's Chewy Chocolate Cookies

This recipe makes 3 dozen
2/3 cup shortening
1-1/2 cups packed brown sugar
1 tblsp water
1 tsp. vanilla ext.
2 eggs
1-1/2 cups all-purpose-flour

1/3 cup unsweetened cocoa-powder
1/2 tsp. salt
1/4 tsp. baking-soda
2 cups semi-sweet chocolate-chips
1/2 cup chopped walnuts

Directions
In large bowl cream shortening, sugar, water and vanilla ext.
Beat in eggs. In a separate bowl, combine flour, cocoa, salt and baking-soda and gradually add to creamed mixture.
Beat until just blended. Stir in chocolate-chips and nuts.
Distribute by rounded tsp.fuls 2 inches apart on ungreased cookie sheets. Bake at 375 Deg. F (190 Deg. C) for 7 - 9 mins.
Do not let over-bake.
Cool 2 mins. before removing from cookie sheet.

Triple Chocolate Chunk-O Cookie

This recipe makes 3 dozen
1-1/2 cups packed brown-sugar
1 cup butter, softened
1 egg
2 1/4 cups all-purpose-flour
2 tsps. ground style cinnamon
1 tsp. baking-soda
1/2 tsp. salt
1 cup chopped walnuts
4 (1 ounce) squares bitter-sweet chocolate, chopped
4 ounces milk-chocolate, chopped
4 ounces white chocolate, chopped
3 tsps. shortening
3 (1 ounce) squares bitter-sweet-chocolate
3 ounces milk-chocolate
3 ounces white-chocolate

Directions
Pre-heat oven to 375 Deg. F (190 Deg. C).

Add in 1 egg and mix well.
Stir in 2 ¼ cups of flour along with cinnamon, salt & baking-soda.
Mix in nuts and the 4 Ozs. of the bitter-sweet, milk & white chocolates.
Drop dough by rounded tblspfuls about 2in. apart on to ungreased cookie sheets.
Bake @ 375 Deg. F (190 Deg. C) for 8 - 10 mins. or until light golden brown.
Cool the dip the cookies in to the chocolate glazing.

Making 3 Chocolate Glaze:

Heat up 1 tsp. of shortening along with bitter-sweet chocolate over a low heat setting remembering to stir constantly - until chocolate melts and becomes smooth.
Remove heat the dip cookies 1/2 inch down in to chocolate along one of the edges.
Repeat with all of the remaining shortening & chocolates.
Rotate the dipped edges of the cookie for each type chocolate.

Jimmy's Chocolate Chip Cookies

This recipe makes 7 dozen
2 cups butter
2 cups packed brown sugar
2 cups white sugar
4 eggs
1 tsp. vanilla ext.
5 cups rolled oats
4 cups all-purpose-flour
2 tsps. baking-powder
2 tsps. baking-soda
1 cup milk-chocolate-chips
3 cups dark chocolate-chips
12 (1 Oz.) squares of German sweet-chocolate (chopped).
Directions
Pre-heat oven to 375 Deg. F (190 Deg. C).

Blend 2 cups of butter, sugar, 4 eggs & vanilla. In a blender and chop the oats until they are fine in texture and size.
Then, using a separate bowl, put in the chopped oatmeal with your flour, baking-powder & baking-soda.

Add flour mixture to butter mixture. Gradually add in chopped milk-chocolate-chips & whole chocolate-chips.
Roll dough in to 1-1/2 inch size balls.
Press with fork. Bake for 6 to 8 mins.
Do not let over-bake.
When they come out of the oven, the cookies will be soft.
Place a chunk of chocolate in the center.

Chocolate Macaroons

This recipe makes 3 dozen
3 egg whites
1 pinch salt
3/4 cup white sugar
1-1/2 cups semi-sweet chocolate-chips
2 1/4 cups shredded coconut
1/2 cup chopped walnuts
1 tsp. vanilla ext.

Directions
Pre-heat oven to 325 Deg. F (165 Deg. C). Grease your cookie sheets.
Melt chocolate over low heat and let cool.
Using a large glass bowl, whip up egg 3 whites until they become foamy.
Slowly add a pich of salt and ¾ cup of sugar - a little at a time, until the mix stands in peaks.
Stir in vanilla. Fold in the chocolate, coconut & nuts.
Drop by tsp.fuls about 2 in. apart on cookie sheets.
Bake 10 - 12 mins. Cookies should be soft in the middle.

Megan's Chocolate Chip Oatmeal Cookies

This recipe makes 15 cookies
2 cups all-purpose-flour
1/2 tsp. baking-soda
1/4 tsp. salt
1 cup rolled oats
1 cup unsalted butter, softened
1 1/3 cups packed dark brown sugar
2 eggs
2 tsps. vanilla ext.
2 cups semi-sweet chocolate-chips
TIME TO PREP
5 mins
COOK
21 mins
READY TO SERVE IN
26 mins

Directions

Pre-heat your oven to 300 Deg. F (150 Deg. C).
Grease your cookie sheets.
Stir together the flour, baking-soda, salt and oats; set aside.
In a medium volume bowl, cream together the butter and brown sugar until smooth.
Beat in the eggs one-by-one then stir in the vanilla.
Mix in the dry ingredients until completely blended before stirring in the chocolate-chips.
Drop by generous spoonfuls on to the prepped cookie sheet at least 3 inches apart. Flatten cookies to 1/2 inch thick.
Bake for 21 mins. in the pre-heated oven, until slightly browned.
Allow the hot cookies to cool down on your baking sheet for 5 mins. before moving over to a wire rack to finish cooling down completely.

Giant Crisp Chocolate Chip Cookies

This recipe makes 2 dozen

2 cups all-purpose-flour
1 tsp. baking-soda
1 tsp. salt
1 cup butter
1-1/2 cups white sugar
1 egg
1 tsp. vanilla ext.
2 cups semi-sweet chocolate-chips
1 cup chopped walnuts
TIME TO PREP
10 mins
COOK
25 mins
READY TO SERVE IN
35 mins

Directions

Pre-heat oven to 350 Deg. F (180 Deg. C). Mix flour, baking-soda and salt; set aside.

In a large volume bowl, cream together the butter and sugar until light & fluffy.

Beat in the egg, then stir in the vanilla. Mix in the dry ingredients until completely blended.

Stir in the chocolate-chips and walnuts.

Roll the dough in to 2 inch balls and place them 3 inches apart on to ungreased cookie sheets.

Bake for 20 to 23 mins. in the pre-heated oven.

Allow cookies to cool for a few mins. on the baking sheet before moving over to a wire rack to finish cooling down completely.

White Chocolate &Macadamia Nut

This recipe makes 3 dozen
1/2 cup butter, softened
3/4 cup packed brown sugar
1/2 cup shortening
1/2 cup white sugar

1 egg
1-1/2 tsps. vanilla ext.
2 cups all-purpose-flour
1 tsp. baking-soda
1/2 tsp. salt
1 cup white chocolate-chips
7 ounces macadamia nuts, chopped
TIME TO PREP
15 mins
COOK
10 mins
READY TO SERVE IN
25 mins

Directions

Pre-heat oven to 350 Deg. F (180 Deg. C). Lightly Grease your cookie sheets.
Beat butter and shortening until soft and creamy. Gradually add the sugars and beat well.
Add egg and vanilla and beat well.
Combine flour, soda and salt; gradually add to butter mixture beating well after each addition.
Stir in chips and nuts.
Drop dough by rounded tsp.fuls on to lightly greased cookie sheets.
Bake for 10-12 mins. or until done.
Remove to wire cooling racks to cool.

Chocolate Chip Cookies (Gluten Free)

This recipe makes 3 dozen
3/4 cup butter, softened
1-1/4 cups packed brown sugar
1/4 cup white sugar
1 tsp. gluten-free vanilla ext.
1/4 cup egg substitute
2 1/4 cups gluten-free baking mix

1 tsp. baking-soda
1 tsp. baking-powder
1 tsp. salt
12 ounces semi-sweet chocolate-chips

Directions

Pre-heat oven to 375 Deg. F (190 Deg. C). TIME TO Prepare a greased baking sheet.

In a medium volume bowl, cream butter and sugar. Gradually add replacer eggs and vanilla while mixing.
Sift together gluten- free flour mix, baking-soda, baking-powder, and salt. Stir in to the butter mixture until blended.
Finally, stir in the chocolate-chips.
Using a tsp., drop cookies 2 inches apart on prepped baking sheet.
Bake in pre-heated oven for 6 to 8 mins. or until light-brown.
Let cookies cool on baking sheet for 2 mins. before removing to wire cooling racks.

All Time Great Chocolate Chip Cookie

This recipe makes 2 dozen
2 1/2 cups all-purpose-flour
1 tsp. baking-soda
1/2 tsp. salt
1 cup vegetable oil
1 cup packed brown sugar
1/2 cup white sugar
2 eggs
1 tsp. vanilla ext.
1 tsp. almond ext.
1 cup semi-sweet chocolate-chips
TIME TO PREP
10 mins
COOK

10 mins
READY TO SERVE IN
30 mins
Directions
Pre-heat oven to 350 Deg. F. (175 Deg. C).
Stir together the flour, baking-soda and salt; set aside.
In a large volume bowl, cream together the vegetable oil, brown & white sugar until smooth.
Beat the eggs in to the mix one-by-one then add in vanilla and almond ext.s.
Blend in the dry ingredients, then fold in the chocolate-chips.
Distribute by rounded spoon-fuls on to an ungreased cookie-sheet..
Bake for 8 - 10 mins. in the pre-heated oven.
Allow the hot cookies to cool down on your baking sheet for 5 mins. before moving over to a wire rack to finish cooling down completely.

America's Best Chocolate Chip Cookies

This recipe makes 3 1/2 dozen
2 1/4 cups all-purpose-flour
1 tsp. baking-soda
1/2 tsp. salt
1 cup unsalted butter, softened
3/4 cup white sugar
2 eggs
2 tsps. Vanilla ext.
2 cups jumbo semi-sweet chocolate-chips
1 cup white chocolate-chips
1-1/2 cups chopped walnuts
TIME TO PREP
20 mins
COOK
10 mins
READY TO SERVE IN

30 mins
Directions
Pre-heat your oven to 375 Deg. F (190 Deg. C
Sift the flour together with the baking-soda & salt then set it aside.
In a large volume bowl, cream the butter and sugar together until smooth. Beat in the eggs, one-by-one then stir in the vanilla.
Blend in the sifted ingredients to form a soft dough. Stir in the chocolate-chips, white chocolate-chips and walnuts.
Drop by heaping tsp.fuls about 2 inches apart on to ungreased baking sheets.
Bake for 8 to 11 mins. in the pre-heated oven, or until lightly golden.
Allow the hot cookies to cool down on your baking sheet for 5 mins. before moving over to a wire rack to finish cooling down completely.

Peanut-Butter Chews

This recipe makes 3 dozen
1 cup cornsyrup
1 cup white sugar
1 cup creamy peanut-butter
4 1/2 cups cornflakes cereal
1 cup semi-sweet chocolate-chips (optional)
1 cup butterscotch chips (optional)
TIME TO PREP
25 mins
READY TO SERVE IN
55 mins
Directions
In a large saucepan over medium heat, combine cornsyrup and white sugar.

Bring to a boil, boil for one minute, and remove from heat. Stir in peanut-butter until completely blended. Mix in cereal until evenly coated.

Drop evenly by spoonfuls on to waxpaper.

In a glass bowl in the microwave, or using a double-boiler, melt chocolate-chips and butterscotch chips, stirring frequently until smooth.

Drizzle on the top of the cookies.

Adam's Dirt Cookies

This recipe makes 4 dozen
2 1/4 cups all-purpose-flour
1 tsp. baking-soda
1 tsp. salt
1 cup white sugar
1/2 cup packed brown sugar
1 cup butter, softened
2 eggs
1 tsp. vanilla ext.
1-1/2 cups chocolate sandwich cookie crumbs
TIME TO PREP
10 mins
COOK
20 mins
READY TO SERVE IN
1 hr 30 mins

Directions

Sift together the flour, baking-soda, and salt. Set aside. In a medium volume bowl, cream the white sugar, brown sugar, and the butter together until smooth.

Add in eggs with your vanilla. Add the flour mixture, and stir until totally combined.

Stir the crushed cookies in to the dough. Cover, and chill the dough for 1/2 hour.

Pre-heat your oven to 375 Deg. F (190 Deg. C). Grease your cookie sheets.
Drop dough by rounded spoonfuls on to prepared cookie sheets. Bake for 10 to 11 mins. in the pre-heated oven. Remove to cool on wire cooling racks.

Chocolate Chip Peppermint Cookies

This recipe makes 30 cookies
3/4 cup butter
1/2 cup white sugar
1/2 cup packed brown sugar
1 egg
1 tsp. vanilla ext.
1 tsp. peppermint ext.
1-1/2 cups all-purpose-flour
1/4 cup unsweetened cocoa-powder
1 tsp. baking-soda
1/4 tsp. salt
1 cup semi-sweet chocolate-chips
TIME TO PREP
15 mins
COOK
12 mins
READY TO SERVE IN
50 mins

Directions

Pre-heat oven to 350 Deg. F. (175 Deg. C). Grease your cookie sheets.
In a large volume bowl, cream together butter, white sugar, and brown sugar until light & fluffy.
Beat in egg, then stir in vanilla and peppermint ext.s.
Combine flour, cocoa powder, baking-soda, and salt; gradually stir it all in to the creamed mix.
Mix in the chocolate-chips. Distribute by rounded spoonfuls on to the prepared cookie sheets.

Bake for 12 to 15 mins. in the pre-heated oven.

Allow cookies to cool on cookie sheets for 5 mins. before transferring to a wire rack to cool completely.

Egg Free Chocolate Chip Pumpkin Cookies

This recipe makes 8 -10 dozen
2 cups white sugar
1 cup shortening
1 (15 ounce) can pumpkin puree
2 tsps. vanilla ext.
4 cups all-purpose-flour
2 tsps. baking-soda
2 tsps. ground style cinnamon
12 ounces semi-sweet chocolate-chips

Directions

Pre-heat oven to 375 Deg. F (190 Deg. C).

Cream the sugar, pumpkin & vanilla as well as the shortening all together. Mix until lwell combined.

Mix the flour, baking-soda and ground style cinnamon. Stir the flour mixture in to the creamed mixture.

Mix until combined. Stir in the chocolate-chips.

Drop by tsps. on to an ungreased baking sheet. Bake at 375 Deg. F (190 Deg. C) for 12 to 15 mins. or until set. Let cookies cool on a rack.

Cake Mix Cookies

This recipe makes 2 dozen
1 (18.25 ounce) package yellow cake mix
1/3 cup vegetable oil
2 eggs
2 cups semi-sweet chocolate-chips

Directions

Pre-heat oven to 350 Deg. F. (175 Deg. C).
Grease your cookie sheets.

Pour cake mix in to a large bowl. Stir in the oil and eggs until completely blended.

Mix in chocolate-chips. Drop dough by tsp.fuls on to the prepared cookie sheets.

Bake for 8 - 10 mins. in the pre-heated oven.

Remove from pan to cool on wire cooling racks.

Award Winning Soft Chocolate Chip Cookies

This recipe makes 6 dozen
4 1/2 cups all-purpose-flour
2 tsps. baking-soda
2 cups butter, softened
1-1/2 cups packed brown sugar
1/2 cup white sugar
2 (3.4 ounce) packages instant vanilla pudding mix
4 eggs
2 tsps. Vanilla ext.
4 cups semi-sweet chocolate-chips
2 cups chopped walnuts (optional)

TIME TO PREP
15 mins
COOK
12 mins
READY TO SERVE IN
1 hr 40 mins

Directions

Pre-heat oven to 350 Deg. F. (175 Deg. C). Sift flour together with the baking-soda then set aside.

Using a good sized bowl, cream the butter, brown and white sugars.

Blend together with instant pudding and mix well until blended. Add in eggs with your vanilla.

Blend in your flour mix. Finally dump in the nuts and chocolate-chips.

Distribute out cookies by the round spoonful on to un-greased cookie sheet.
Bake for around 10 - 12 mins. in your pre-heated oven.
Edges should appear to be golden-brown.

Best Chocolate Chip Cookies

This recipe makes 4 dozen
1 cup butter, softened
1 cup white sugar
1 cup packed brown sugar
2 eggs
2 tsps. Vanilla ext.
3 cups all-purpose-flour
1 tsp. baking-soda
2 tsps. Hot water
1/2 tsp. salt
2 cups semi-sweet chocolate-chips
1 cup chopped walnuts
TIME TO PREP
20 mins
COOK
10 mins
READY TO SERVE IN
1 hr

Directions
Pre-heat oven to 350 Deg. F. (175 Deg. C).
Cream in your butter along with white and brown sugars until everything is smooth.
Beat the eggs in to the mix one-by-one then add in vanilla. Dissolve the baking-soda in some hot water.
Add batter together with your salt. Stir in the flour along with chocolate-chips & nuts.
Distribute in generous spoonfuls on to an ungreased pan.
Bake for aprox. 10 mins in a pre-heated oven or until the cookie edges are golden browned.

Puffy Chocolaty Chip Cookies

This recipe makes 3 dozen
2 1/4 cups all-purpose-flour
1/2 cup unsweetened cocoa-powder
1 tsp. baking-soda
1/4 tsp. salt
1 cup butter
3/4 cup packed brown sugar
1/3 cup white sugar
1 tsp. vanilla ext.
2 eggs
2 cups semi-sweet chocolate-chips

Directions
Pre-heat oven to 350 Deg. F (180 Deg. C).
Mix together flour, cocoa, baking-soda and salt.
Cream margarine, both sugars, and vanilla until creamy.
Beat in eggs 1 at a time, beating 1 1/2 mins. after each addition.
Beat in the flour mixture. Stir in the chocolate-chips.
Drop by tblsp on to ungreased cookie sheets.

Bake for 8 - 10 mins. or until puffy. Centers will be soft.
Let stand on cookie sheets for 2 mins., then remove to wire cooling racks to cool completely.

Absolutely Excellent Oatmeal Cookies

This recipe makes 7 dozen
1 cup shortening
2 cups brown sugar
3 eggs
1 cup sour milk
1 tsp. vanilla ext.
3 cups all-purpose-flour
1 tsp. baking-powder
1 tsp. baking-soda

1/2 tsp. salt
1 tsp. ground style cinnamon
2 cups rolled oats
1 cup chopped walnuts
1 cup raisins
1 cup semi-sweet chocolate-chips
TIME TO PREP
20 mins
COOK
12 mins
READY TO SERVE IN
2 hrs

Directions

Pre-heat oven to 350 Deg. F. (175 Deg. C). Grease your cookie sheets.

In a large volume bowl, cream the shortening and sugar until light & fluffy.

Add the eggs one-by-one, beating well with each addition, then stir in the vanilla and sour milk.

Combine the flour, baking-powder, baking-soda, salt and cinnamon, gradually stir it all in to the creamed mix.

Finally, stir in the rolled oats, and your choice of additions. Distribute by rounded spoonfuls on to the prepped cookie sheets.

Bake for 12 to 15 mins. in the pre-heated oven.

Allow the hot cookies to cool down on your baking sheet for 5 mins. before moving over to a wire rack to finish cooling down completely.

Chocolaty Marshmallow Cookies

This recipe makes 5 dozen
1/2 cup butter
2 (1 ounce) squares unsweetened-chocolate
1 egg
1 cup packed brown sugar

1 tsp. vanilla ext.
1/2 tsp. baking-soda
1-1/2 cups all-purpose-flour
1/2 cup milk
1 (16 Oz.) pkg. large marshmallows

Directions

Pre-heat oven to 350 Deg. F(180 Deg. C). Lightly Grease a cookie sheet or you may line with parchment paper.

Melt butter & chocolate in small sauce-pan using a low heat; stir-to-blend then remove from heat and let cool.

Beat egg, vanilla, brown sugar and baking-soda in large bowl until light & fluffy.

Blend in the chocolate mixture with 1 ½ cups of flour until smooth.

Beat in ½ cup of milk to make a light, cake-batter-consistency dough.

Lay out the dough in tsp.fuls 2 inches apart on a prepped cookie sheets.

Bake 10 - 12 mins. (Should be firm in center at this point).

Cut all the marshmallows in to halves and place each half cut side down on to a baked cookie.

Return to oven 1 minute (or until marshmallow is hot enough to stick to the cookie).

Remove cookies over to bake racks to cool.

Cherry Mountain Chocolate Cookies

This recipe makes 24 cookies
1 cup all-purpose-flour
1/4 cup unsweetened cocoa-powder
1 tsp. baking-powder
1/4 tsp. salt
1/2 cup unsalted butter, softened
1 cup white sugar
1 egg
1 tsp. instant coffee granules

1 tsp. vanilla ext.
1/4 cup miniature semi-sweet chocolate-chips
1/4 cup white chocolate-chips
1 cup dried cherries

TIME TO PREP
15 mins
COOK
10 mins
READY TO SERVE IN
25 mins

Directions

Pre-heat an oven to 350 Deg. F. (175 Deg. C).
Line two large baking sheets with parchment paper.
Combine flour, cocoa powder, baking-powder, and salt in a bowl.
Beat the butter and sugar together In a large volume bowl with a mixer set on medium-high speed, until light & fluffy.
Beat the egg, coffee granules, and vanilla in to the butter and sugar mixture until blended.
Switch the speed to low & pour in the flour mixture. Beat until totally combined.
Stir in semi-sweet chocolate-chips, white chocolate-chips, and dried cherries.
Drop spoonfuls of the dough two inches apart on to the Prepped baking sheets.
Bake 10 to 12 mins. per batch in the pre-heated oven, until cookies are just becoming firm.
Let cool on baking sheets for two mins.
Transfer cookies to a wire rack to let cool completely.

Best Big, Fat, Chewy Chocolate Chip Cookie

This recipe makes 1-1/2 dozen
2 cups all-purpose-flour
1/2 tsp. baking-soda
1/2 tsp. salt
3/4 cup unsalted butter, melted
1 cup packed brown sugar
1/2 cup white sugar
1 tblsp vanilla ext.
1 egg
1 egg yolk
2 cups semi-sweet chocolate-chips
TIME TO PREP
10 mins
COOK
15 mins
READY TO SERVE IN
40 mins

Directions

Pre-heat your oven to 325 Deg. F (165 Deg. C).
Grease a cookie sheet or you may line with parchment paper.
Sift the flour together with the baking-soda & salt then set it aside.
Using a medium sized bowl cream the melted butter along with the brown and white sugars until everything is completely blended.
Beat the vanilla in alongside of the egg and yolk until it becomes light and creamy. Mix your sifted ingredients together until they're completely blended.
Using a wooden spoon manually blend in the chocolate-chips.
Deposit your cookie dough about 1/4 cup at a time on to a pre greased cookie sheet.
Cookies should be spaced out roughly three inches apart.

Bake for 15 - 17 mins. using a pre-heated oven until the edges are slightly toasted. Cool on your baking sheet for a few mins before moving everything over to wire rack to finish cooling

Chocolate Jumbo

This recipe makes 4 dozen
1/2 cup shortening
1/2 cup white sugar
1 cup molasses
1 egg
2 1/2 cups all-purpose-flour
1/4 cup unsweetened cocoa-powder
1/2 tsp. ground style cinnamon
1/2 tsp. ground cloves
1/2 tsp. ground allspice
1 tsp. baking-soda
1 pinch salt
1/2 cup hot water
48 walnut halves

Directions

Pre-heat oven to 375 Deg. F (190 Deg. C).
Cream shortening and sugar together.
Add 1 egg with molasses and mix well.
Sift together dry ingredients, add to shortening mixture, alternating with hot water. Mix well.
Distribute by rounded tsps. on to ungreased cookie sheet. Bake 8-10 mins.
Remove from cookie sheet, cool.
Frost with a butter frosting and finish off by topping each cookie with a walnut.

Maggie's Camper Specials

This recipe makes 5 dozen cookies
1 cup butter
1-1/2 cups white sugar

1 cup packed brown sugar
2 eggs
1 tsp. vanilla ext.
2 tsps. Instant-espresso powder
1 3/4 cups all-purpose-flour
1 tsp. baking-soda
3 cups old-fashioned oats
1-1/2 cups salted peanuts
1 1/3 cups milk-chocolate-chips
1/2 cup flaked coconut
TIME TO PREP
15 mins
COOK
12 mins
READY TO SERVE IN
27 mins

Directions
Pre-heat your oven to 350 Deg. F. (175 Deg. C).
Using a good sized bowl, cream the butter, brown and white sugars until smooth.
Beat the eggs in to the mix one-by-one then add in vanilla and espresso powder.
Combine the flour and baking-soda; blend in to the sugar mixture until just moist.
Stir in the oats, peanuts, chocolate-chips and coconut until evenly mixed.
Drop by heaping tsp.-fuls on to an ungreased cookie-sheet.
Bake for 12 mins. in the pre-heated oven, or until the edges are golden.
Let cool for 5 mins. on the baking sheets before removing to wire bake rack to cool completely.

Killer Chocolate Chip Cookie

This recipe makes 3 - 4 dozen
1-1/2 cups butter flavor shortening

2 1/2 cups packed brown sugar
2 eggs
2 tsps. salt
4 tblsps milk
2 tblsps vanilla ext.
3 1/2 cups all-purpose-flour
1-1/2 tsps. baking-soda
2 cups semi-sweet chocolate-chips
1 cup chopped walnuts

Directions

Cream sugar in to shortening. Add milk and vanilla beat until fluffy

Blend in egg. Then add dry ingredients and mix well. Stir in chips and nuts.

Drop by tsp. on to greased baking sheets and bake at 350 Deg. F. (175 Deg. C) for 8-10 mins. for chewy cookies or 10-13 mins. for crispy cookies.

ENJOY!!!

Dr. Goodcookie

This recipe makes 4 dozen cookies
5 (1 ounce) squares semi-sweet chocolate, chopped
1 cup butter, softened
1-1/2 cups white sugar
4 eggs
2 tsps. vanilla ext.
1/2 cup peanut-butter
4 cups all-purpose-flour
2 tsps. baking-soda
2 tsps. baking-powder
1 tsp. salt
1 (3.9 ounce) package instant chocolate pudding mix
2 cups rolled oats
2 cups chopped peanut-butter cups
TIME TO PREP

15 mins
COOK
10 mins
READY TO SERVE IN
30 mins

Directions

Pre-heat oven to 350 Deg. F. (175 Deg. C). Grease your cookie sheets. In the microwave or in a metal bowl over a pan of simmering water, melt the semi-sweet chocolate, stirring frequently until smooth.

Remove from heat and set aside to cool slightly.

In a large volume bowl, cream the butter and sugar together until smooth.

Beat 4 eggs one-by-one, then stir in the vanilla.

Mix in the melted chocolate and peanut-butter.

Sift together the flour, baking-soda, baking-powder, salt and instant pudding mix; gradually blend in to the peanut-butter mixture. Stir in the oats and chopped peanut butter cups.

Drop by generous spoonfuls on to the prepped cookie sheets.

Bake for 8 - 10 mins. in the pre-heated oven. Allow cookies to sit and cool on baking sheet for 5 mins. before moving over to a bake rack to finish cooling down completely.

No Peeking!

This recipe makes 4 - 5 dozen
4 egg whites
1 pinch salt
1 dash cream of tartar
1 1/3 cups white sugar
4 drops green food coloring
1 cup semi-sweet chocolate-chips
1/2 tsp. peppermint ext.

Directions

Pre-heat oven to 350 Deg. F. (175 Deg. C). Grease 2 cookie sheets.

Beat egg whites until they are fluffy.
Add in salt & cream-of-tartar. Adding in the sugar gradually as you go.
Continue beating until egg whites until they are stiff and will stand up.
Fold in chosen food colorings & peppermint ext. as well as chocolate-chips.
Drop by tsp.fuls on to the pre-greased sheets and place in to oven then turn oven OFF.
Leave undisturbed inside the oven overnight.
Resist the urge to open the oven after cookies have been inserted (hence the name!) or they will become soggy.

Chewy Chocolate Chip Oatmeal Cookies

This recipe makes 3 1/2 dozen
1 cup butter, softened
1 cup packed light-brown sugar
1/2 cup white sugar
2 eggs
2 tsps. Vanilla ext.
1-1/4 cups all-purpose-flour
1/2 tsp. baking-soda
1 tsp. salt
3 cups quick-cooking oats
1 cup chopped walnuts
1 cup semi-sweet chocolate-chips
TIME TO PREP
15 mins
COOK
12 mins
READY TO SERVE IN
55 mins
Directions
Pre-heat your oven to 325 Deg. F (165 Deg. C).

Using a good sized bowl, cream the butter, brown and white sugars until smooth.

Beat in your eggs one by one & then stir in vanilla. Combine the flour, baking-soda, and salt; stir it all in to the creamed mix until just blended.
Mix in some quick oats, chocolate-chips and walnuts. Drop by generous spoonfuls on to ungreased baking sheets.
Bake for 12 mins. in the pre-heated oven.
Allow cookies to cool on baking-sheet for apx. 5 mins before moving over to a baking rack to finish cooling.

Chocolaty Chocolate Chip Cookies 1.0

This recipe makes 4 dozen
1 cup butter, softened
1-1/2 cups white sugar
2 eggs
2 tsps. Vanilla ext.
2 cups all-purpose-flour
2/3 cup cocoa powder
3/4 tsp. baking-soda
1/4 tsp. salt
2 cups semi-sweet chocolate-chips
1/2 cup chopped walnuts (optional)
TIME TO PREP
15 mins
COOK
10 mins
READY TO SERVE IN
45 mins
Directions
Pre-heat oven to 350 Deg. F. (175 Deg. C).
Using a larger sized bowl, blend together eggs, sugar, butter and vanilla until mix is light & fluffy.

Combine the flour, cocoa, baking-soda, and salt; stir in to the butter mix until it's completely blended.
Mix in the chocolate-chips & (optional) walnuts.
Distribute by rounded tsp.-fuls on to an ungreased cookie-sheet.
Bake for 8 - 10 mins. in the pre-heated oven, or just until set.
Cool for a minute on the cookie sheets then move over to wire rack to finish cooling.

Part 2

Introduction

To most people, chocolate is a very special treat. One simply cannot live through life without having eaten a chocolate.
The main types of chocolate are white, milk, dark, and unsweetened. The flavor and texture of the chocolate is affected by how it is manufactured.
White chocolate doesn't contain any cacao solids, only cacao butter, but it is still considered a chocolate.
Milk chocolate is a sweet type of chocolate that is usually used for confectionery or candy making.
Dark chocolate doesn't contain milk and it is mostly used for baking purposes.
Unsweetened chocolate is very bitter and has 100% cacao content.
Surely, there is a type of chocolate for everyone to enjoy. Whether it is in the form of a hot drink or as an ingredient in cake, chocolate brings us a special kind of joy that no other food can. So, start reading this cookbook and find the recipe that best suits your taste or the occasion.
Let's get started!

Ultimate Dark Chocolate Cake

If you are a chocolate lover and looking for a delicious cake recipe, this is the perfect recipe for you!
Preparation time: 10 minutes
Total time: 1 hour 45 minutes
Yield: 10 servings

Ingredients
1 1/2 cups (150 g) unsweetened cocoa powder
1 tablespoon (12 g) baking powder
1 1/2 teaspoons (9 g) baking soda
2 1/2 cups (315 g) flour
1 1/2 teaspoons (7.5 g) salt
2 cups (440 g) sugar
1/2 cup (125 ml) vegetable oil
1 1/2 teaspoons (7.5 ml) vanilla extract
3 (60 g) whole eggs
1 cup (250 g) applesauce
1 1/2 cups (375 ml) hot water
Chocolate Butter Frosting:
1 stick (120 g) butter, sliced into cubes
1 cup (100 g) pure icing sugar, sifted
6 oz. (180 g) dark chocolate, melted and cooled

Method

1. Preheat your oven to 350°F. Line 2 (8-inch round) cake pans with parchment paper.
2. Sift together the cocoa powder with the baking soda, baking powder, flour, salt, and sugar in a large mixing bowl.
3. Add in the oil, vanilla extract, eggs, buttermilk, and hot water.
4. With a mixer set at low speed, mix everything together until it becomes smooth.
5. Pour your batter equally into prepared cake pans. Bake them for about 45 minutes. You can check if it's cooked by sticking a toothpick or wooden skewer down the middle of the cake. If it comes out clean, then it's done.
6. Allow the cakes to cool for about 20 minutes in wire racks. Turn them upside down and gently allow them to fall off the pans. Remove the parchment paper. Cool once again.
7. Meanwhile, put the butter in a large bowl. Beat for 2 minutes using an electric mixer. Slowly and gradually add the icing sugar and beat until the mixture looks light and fluffy. Add the melted chocolate. Stir together very rapidly until smooth and well combined.
8. Frost the top part of the bottom cake using a spatula then put the other cake on top of it. Frost everything, from sides to the top. Cut into 8-10 slices.
9. Serve and enjoy.

Nutritional Information:

Energy - 501 calories
Fat - 24.1 g
Carbohydrates - 70.3 g
Protein - 7.8 g
Sodium - 6.9 mg

Oozing Chocolate Lava Cake

You're going to want to have seconds. These mini-cakes are to die for!
Preparation Time: 10 minutes
Total Time: 1 hour 20 minutes
Yield: 4 servings
Ingredients
2 (20 g) egg yolks
2 (60 g) whole eggs
3 tablespoons (45 g) white sugar
4 oz. (120 g) chopped dark chocolate, melted
1/4 cup (60 g) unsalted butter, melted
1/4 teaspoon (1.5 ml) vanilla extract
4 teaspoons (10 g) unsweetened cocoa powder
3 tablespoons (20 g) flour
pinch of salt
cooking oil spray
icing sugar, to serve
Method
1. Spray ramekins with oil thoroughly.
2. In a medium bowl, beat the eggs and sugar. It should come out looking really foamy.
3. Stir in the melted chocolate, butter, and vanilla extract.
4. Now, sift the cocoa powder, flour, and salt into the combined chocolate-egg mixture. Stir everything together to form a batter.

5. Pour and divide your batter between each ramekin evenly.
6. Chill the chocolate batter for 30 minutes then preheat your oven to 425°F.
7. Place your cooled ramekins into a deep dish or baking pan and pour some hot water in it to reach the sides of the ramekins. Make sure that the water doesn't go inside the ramekins, otherwise you'd ruin your batter.
8. Bake in your oven for 15-20 minutes.
9. Allow to cool for about 15 minutes then carefully take them out of their ramekins. Sprinkle some icing sugar for a nice touch.
10. Serve and enjoy.

Nutritional Information:

Energy - 371 calories
Fat - 24.7 g
Carbohydrates - 31.8 g
Protein - 7.4 g
Sodium - 178 mg

Chocolate And Coffee Cake

If you are looking for a cake recipe that combines the flavor of chocolate and coffee, this is the perfect recipe for you. Surely, the best of both worlds!

Preparation time: 10 minutes
Total time: 1 hour
Yield: 12 servings

Ingredients
1 3/4 cups (220 g) flour
2 cups (440 g) brown sugar
3/4 cup (75 g) unsweetened cocoa powder
2 teaspoons (12 g) baking soda
1 teaspoon (4 g) baking powder
1 teaspoon (5 g) salt
2 (60 g) whole eggs
1 cup (250 ml) strong brewed coffee, cooled
1 cup (250 ml) applesauce
1/2 cup (60 ml) vegetable oil
1 teaspoon (5 ml) vanilla extract
chocolate frosting, to serve
chocolate chips, to serve

Method
1. Preheat your oven to 350°F. Line a 13 x 9-inch cake pan with parchment paper and sprinkle some flour. Set aside.

2. Combine the flour, sugar, cocoa powder, baking powder, baking soda, and salt in a large bowl. Make a well in the center.
3. Place the eggs, the coffee, buttermilk, oil, and vanilla extract in the well that you made then mix everything together for 2 minutes on the medium setting. Pour and divide into both pans.
4. Bake for about 45 minutes to an hour or until tested done. Allow to cool in wire rack, then take it out of the pan gently and remove the parchment paper.
5. Put frosting and chocolate chips on top. Cut into 10 slices.
6. Serve and enjoy.

Nutritional Information:
Energy - 273 calories
Fat - 10.8 g
Carbohydrates - 43.1 g
Protein - 4.1 g
Sodium - 426 mg

Easy Dark Chocolate Cake

This chocolate cake taste heavenly. It is best served with coffee or tea.

Preparation time: 10 minutes
Total Time: 55 minutes
Yield: 12 servings

Ingredients
1 1/2 cups (330 g) brown sugar
3/4 cup (75 g) cocoa powder, unsweetened
1 1/2 teaspoons (9 g) baking soda
2 cups (250 g) flour
1 teaspoon (2 g) cinnamon, ground
3/4 teaspoon (4 g) salt
1 1/2 teaspoons (7.5 ml) vanilla extract
3/4 cup (185 ml) vegetable oil
1 (60 g) whole egg
1 1/2 cups (375 ml) water
1 1/2 teaspoons (7.5 ml) vinegar
dark chocolate frosting, ready made

Method
1. Preheat your oven to 350°F.
2. Sift all of your dry ingredients in a large bowl then add the liquids. Combine everything together until smooth then pour into an ungreased 9 x 13-inch pan.

3. Bake for about 30-40 minutes or until tested done. Take it out and allow to cool in wire rack.
4. Frost with dark chocolate icing. Cut into 10 slices.
5. Serve and enjoy.

Nutritional Information:

Energy - 285 calories
Fat - 14.9 g
Carbohydrates - 36.9 g
Protein - 3.7 g
Sodium - 319 mg

Chocolate Mousse Cake

Delicious and creamy, this cake is sure to please!
Preparation time: 20 minutes
Total time: 2 hours 2 minutes
Yield: 10 servings

Ingredients
8 ounces (250 g) bittersweet chocolate (chopped)
1/4 cup (60 g) unsalted butter
12 (20 g) egg yolks
12 (40 g) egg whites
1/3 cup (75 g) + 2 tablespoons (30 g) granulated sugar, divided
1 1/4 cups (315 g) heavy cream
1 tablespoon (7 g) unsweetened cocoa powder
cooking oil spray
ready-made chocolate frosting, for topping

Method
1. Preheat your oven to 300°F. Spray a 9-inch spring form pan with oil then line with parchment paper.
2. Heat the chocolate and the unsalted butter in a double boiler. Stir occasionally until the butter melts. Remove from heat and allow to cool slightly.
3. Mix the egg yolks with 1/4 cup of sugar in a bowl until it becomes thick. Pour in the melted chocolate and set aside.

4. In another mixing bowl, beat the egg whites. They should turn foamy. Then, slowly add the 2 tablespoons of sugar. Beat continuously until the mixture forms peaks. Fold 1/3 of the egg whites into the melted chocolate mixture. Fold in the remaining and mix. Pour about 2/3 of the mixture into your baking pan.
5. Bake in the oven for 30-40 minutes. Allow to cool. Take the cake out of the pan and chill for about an hour.
6. Meanwhile, whip the cream into soft peaks in a medium bowl. Fold this into the remaining uncooked chocolate mixture. Cover with cling wrap then chill for at least an hour.
7. When your cake is chilled, take it out along with the mousse and slather the mousse on top of the cake.
8. Spread frosting on top. Cut into 8-10 slices.
9. Serve and enjoy.

Nutritional Information:

Energy - 321 calories
Fat - 22.7 g
Carbohydrates - 22.3 g
Protein - 9.9 g
Sodium - 107 mg

Apple And Chocolate Cake

We know that orange and chocolate go well together, but what most people miss out on is the combined flavors of apple and chocolate!

Preparation time: 15 minutes
Total time: 1 hour 15 minutes
Yield: 12 servings

Ingredients
2 tablespoons (30 g) unsalted butter
1 cup (100 g) caster sugar
3 (60 g) whole eggs
3/4 cup (75 g) cocoa powder
4 tablespoons (60 ml) water
1/2 teaspoon (3 g) baking soda
2 (180 g) green apples, peeled, cored, and quartered
2 cups (250 g) self-raising flour
1 1/2 cups (150 g) powdered sugar
2 tablespoons (15 g) cocoa powder
2 tablespoons (30 g) unsalted butter
2 tablespoons (30 ml) milk
cooking oil spray

Method
1. Preheat the oven to 325°F and grease a 9-inch square cake pan with oil spray.

2. In a food processor, combine the first 8 ingredients. Process everything together just until the mixture becomes smooth and thoroughly combined. Dump the batter into the prepared pan and bake for 45 minutes to an hour, or until tested done.
3. Remove the pan from the oven and allow to cool for 5 minutes. Transfer to a wire rack to cool completely.
4. Put the remaining 4 ingredients in a bowl over a pan of simmering water. Heat it until the butter melts. Stir until it becomes smooth. Add some extra milk if the consistency is a little too stiff.
5. Spread the resulting frosting over the cake. You may chill the cake for a little while to allow the frosting to set. Once the frosting has set, you may then serve the cake.

Nutritional Information:
Energy - 278 calories
Fat - 5.9 g
Carbohydrates - 55.5 g
Protein - 4.6 g
Sodium - 98 mg

Chocolate Mocha Cake

You can frost this awesome cake either with more chocolate or with coffee flavored frosting.

Preparation Time: 10 minutes
Total Time: 45 minutes
Yield: 10 servings

Ingredients
1 tablespoon (7 g) instant coffee powder
1 cup (250 ml) hot water
2 cups (250 g) flour
3/4 cup (75 g) unsweetened cocoa powder
2 cups (440 g) white sugar
2 teaspoons (12 g) baking soda
1 teaspoon (4 g) baking powder
1/2 teaspoon (2.5 g) salt
1/2 cup (125 ml) vegetable oil
1 cup (125 ml) buttermilk
2 (60 g) whole eggs
cooking oil spray
chocolate or coffee-flavored frosting, to serve

Method
1. Grease 2 (9-inch) cake pans with oil spray and preheat your oven to 350°F.
2. Dissolve the coffee powder in the hot water.

3. Combine the flour with cocoa powder, sugar, baking powder, baking soda, salt oil, buttermilk, eggs, in a large bowl.
4. Add the coffee to the mixture and beat at medium speed for about 2 minutes.
5. Pour batter into cake pans. Bake for 30 to 35 minutes. You'll know that it's done when you stick a toothpick in the middle and it comes out clean. Allow to cool in their pans for about 10 minutes then turn upside down to remove cake from pans. Allow to cool completely in wire racks.

*Frost the cake with chocolate or coffee icing then drizzle with melted chocolate for a nice finish.

Nutritional Information:

Energy - 377 calories
Fat - 13.2 g
Carbohydrates - 64.1 g
Protein - 5.9 g
Sodium - 411 mg

Flourless Chocolate Cake

This chocolate cake recipe is perfect for people who are avoiding gluten in their diet.
Preparation time: 15 minutes
Total time: 1 day (including refrigeration)
Yield: 10 servings

Ingredients
1/2 cup (125 ml) water
1/4 teaspoon (1.5 g) salt
3/4 cup (165 g) white sugar
16 squares of bittersweet chocolate (1 oz. or 28 g each), melted
1 stick (120 g) unsalted butter
6 (60 g) whole eggs

Method
1. Grease your cake pan and preheat your oven to 300°F.
2. Combine the salt and sugar with water and heat in a saucepan over medium heat. Keep stirring until the sugar has completely dissolved. Set aside.
3. Pour the melted chocolate into the bowl of an electric mixer. Slice the butter into small pieces. Add the butter into the chocolate while the mixer is turned on. Finally, add the dissolved sugar that you made earlier.

4. Pour the batter into the pan. You're going to cook this cake in a water bath so get a pan that is larger than the pan that contains your batter, fill it up with boiling water, about halfway up the sides of the cake pan. Bake the cake in the water bath in your preheated oven for about 45 minutes to an hour.
5. Take the cake pan out of the oven and cool in wire rack.
6. Chill overnight. This will make the cake set and easy to slice.
7. Serve the next day.

Nutritional Information:
Energy - 415 calories
Fat - 26.8 g
Carbohydrates - 39.2 g
Protein - 6.4 g
Sodium - 161 mg

Chocolate Bundt Cake With Raspberries

The raspberries add an amazing taste to this delightful chocolate Bundt cake.
Preparation time: 15 minutes
Total time: 1 hour 20 minutes
Yield: 10 servings

Ingredients
For the cake:
1 cup (125 g) flour
1 cup (220 g) sugar, divided
1/2 cup (50 g) unsweetened cocoa powder
1/2 teaspoon (3 g) baking soda
1/4 teaspoon (1.5 g) salt
1/3 cup (85 g) unsalted butter, softened
2 tablespoons (30 ml) vegetable oil
2 (60 g) whole eggs
1 teaspoon (5 ml) vanilla extract
1/2 cup (125 ml) water
1/2 cup (80 g) semi-sweet chocolate chips
2 cups (400 g) fresh raspberries
cooking oil spray
For the glaze:
1 cup (160 g) semi-sweet chocolate chips
2/3 cup (165 g) heavy cream
pinch of salt

Method
1. Preheat your oven to 325°F and put a rack in the lower third of it. Grease your Bundt pan with oil spray.
2. Combine the flour, sugar, cocoa powder, baking soda, and salt in a large bowl using a mixer set on low speed. Mix for about a minute. Then, add the eggs, butter, oil, vanilla extract, and water. Continue mixing on low speed until everything is combined.
3. Fold in the ½ cup chocolate chips.
4. Put the batter into your cake pan and put it in the oven for 35 to 40 minutes or until tested done.
5. Remove from the oven and cool slightly for about 10 minutes before taking the cake out. Once the cake is out, cool completely in wire rack.
6. Make the glaze by combining the chocolate chips, heavy cream and salt in a heavy bottomed saucepan. Simmer over medium-low heat until the chocolate has melted.
7. Pour the glaze on top of the cooled cake and put your raspberries in the center (where the hole is).
8. Refrigerate until ready to serve. Cut into 10 slices.
9. Serve and enjoy.

Nutritional Information:
Energy - 368 calories
Fat - 19.9 g
Carbohydrates - 49.7 g
Protein - 5.2 g
Sodium - 182 mg

Moist And Rich Chocolate Cupcake

This chocolate recipe with marshmallows is great for a party dessert or snack!

Preparation time: 15 minutes
Total time: 45 minutes
Yield: 18 servings

Ingredients
1 ½ cups (185 g) all-purpose flour
1 cup (220 g) granulated sugar
1 teaspoon (6 g) baking soda
1 teaspoon (5 g) salt
2/3 cup (70 g) cocoa powder
1 cup (250 ml) hot water
1/2 cup (125 ml) canola oil
1 teaspoon (5 ml) white vinegar

Method
1. Preheat the oven to 350 F. Line the muffin tins with paper cups.
2. In a large bowl, combine flour, baking soda, cocoa powder, sugar and salt.
3. Combine the hot water, canola oil, and vinegar in a separate bowl.
4. Mix together the dry and wet ingredients until just blended and smooth.
5. Spoon batter into the prepared muffin cups, about 2/3 full.

6. Bake in the oven for 20 minutes or until tested done. Place in wire racks to cool.
7. Serve and enjoy.

Nutritional Information:

Energy - 139 calories
Fat - 6.5 g
Carbohydrates - 20.4 g
Protein - 1.5 g
Sodium - 200 mg

Heavenly Brownies

These brownies are a sure hit to adults and kids alike! Perfect for snacks or dessert.

Preparation time: 10 minutes
Total time: 40 minutes
Yield: 12 servings

Ingredients
1/2 cup (120 g) butter
1 cup (220 g) white sugar
2 (60 g) whole eggs
1 teaspoon (5 ml) vanilla extract
1/3 cup (35 g) unsweetened cocoa powder
1/2 cup (60 g) flour
1/2 teaspoon (2 g) baking powder
1/4 teaspoon (1.5 g) salt

Method
1. Preheat your oven to 350°F and grease an 8-inch square pan. Sprinkle flour on the pan once greased.
2. Melt the 1/2 cup of butter in a saucepan over low heat. Remove from heat then add in the sugar, eggs, and vanilla extract. Stir for a bit then add the 1/3 cup of cocoa powder, 1/2 cup of flour, baking powder, and salt.
3. Pour the batter into your baking pan and spread it evenly.

4. Put in the oven and bake for 25 to 30 minutes. Take it out once it's done and allow to cool before cutting into squares.
5. Serve and enjoy.

Nutritional Information:

Energy - 168 calories
Fat - 8.9 g
Carbohydrates - 22.2 g
Protein - 2.1 g
Sodium - 117 mg

Homemade Chocolate Soufflé

This chocolate soufflé recipe is very easy to do and watching it cook is a nice sight to see.

Preparation time: 10 minutes
Total time: 30 minutes
Yield: 2 servings

Ingredients
3 tablespoons (45 g) granulated sugar
2 1/2 ounces (70 g) semisweet chocolate, melted
1 (60 g) whole egg, separated
2 (40 g) egg whites
1/4 teaspoon (1.5 g) salt
1 tablespoon (15 g) heavy cream
1 teaspoon (2.5 g) flour
1/4 teaspoon (0.5 g) ground cinnamon
powdered sugar

Method
1. Preheat your oven to 375°F and place the rack in the middle of it. Grease 2 ramekins with oil spray and then coat the insides with 1 1/2 teaspoons of sugar.
2. In a bowl, mix together the egg yolk and cream. Add in the melted chocolate. Stir until smooth then add the flour and cinnamon.

3. In another bowl, beat the egg whites along with the salt using an electric mixer set on high speed. Soft peaks should form. Beat in the remaining sugar, until stiff peaks form.
4. Pour half of the beaten egg whites into the chocolate mixture then fold the chocolate-egg mixture into the remaining egg whites. Divide mixture into 2 ramekins.
5. Put the ramekins on a baking pan and bake until it is puffed. This should take about 18 to 22 minutes. Once done, dust with some powdered sugar then serve.
6. Enjoy.

Nutritional Information:
Energy - 295 calories
Fat - 13.2 g
Carbohydrates - 42.1 g
Protein - 8.1 g
Sodium - 217 mg

Sumptuous Chocolate Blancmange

This creamy and chocolate-y dessert is a sure hit!
Preparation time: 10 minutes
Total time: 2 hours 10 minutes
Yield: 6 servings
Ingredients
1/4 cup (15 g) cornstarch
3 tablespoons (45 g) granulated sugar
3 tablespoon (20 g) cocoa powder
2 ounces (56 g) bittersweet chocolate, melted
2 cups (250 ml) milk
1 1/2 teaspoons (7.5 g) vanilla extract
Whipped cream, for topping
chocolate syrup, to serve

Method

1. Mix together the cornstarch, cocoa powder, and sugar in a bowl. In a saucepan, whisk in the melted chocolate and milk to the cornstarch mixture. Cook over medium heat. Whisk constantly, but gently. Allow the mixture to boil.
2. Stir in the vanilla extract and pour into your molds. Chill for at least 2 hours.
3. Serve with whipped cream on top and drizzle with chocolate syrup.

4. Enjoy.

Nutritional Information:

Energy - 143 calories
Fat - 4.8 g
Carbohydrates - 22.1 g
Protein - 3.9 g
Sodium - 47 mg

Choco Profiteroles

Delicious and light, these chocolate cream puffs will practically melt in your mouth!
Preparation time: 10 minutes
Total time: 1 hour 10 minutes
Yield: 16 servings

Ingredients
1 cup (250 ml) water
1/2 cup (125 g) butter
1/4 teaspoon (1.5 g) salt
1 cup (125 g) flour
4 (60 g) large eggs
2 cups (250 g) all-purpose cream, divided
1/4 cup (25 g) icing sugar
8 ounces (250 g) dark chocolate, chopped

Method
1. Preheat your oven to 425°F and line your baking pan with parchment paper.
2. Boil the water. Add in the butter and salt, stirring to melt the butter completely. Remove from heat and add the flour. Stir until it becomes smooth.
3. Add the eggs. Stir after adding each egg. Mix well.

4. Spoon about 2 tablespoons of the mixture onto your baking pan with ample space between each one.
5. Put the baking pan into the oven. Bake until the pastries are puffed and turn golden brown. This should take about 18-22 minutes. Remove them from the baking pan and allow to cool in wire rack.
6. **To make the cream filling**: Beat 1 cup of the all-purpose cream. It should form soft peaks. Add the icing and beat further until stiff peaks form. Transfer in a piping bag.
7. Make holes in the middle of each pastry. Fill it with the cream filling.
8. **For the chocolate topping:** Take the remaining cup of cream and put it in a small saucepan and simmer over medium heat for 2 minutes, stirring often. Remove from heat and add the chocolate to melt. Once smooth, set aside.
9. Top each with the melted chocolate sauce.
   Serve and enjoy.

Nutritional Information:
Energy - 195 calories
Fat - 12.8 g
Carbohydrates - 18.0 g
Protein - 2.7 g
Sodium - 104 mg

Easy Rocky Road Bars

This chocolate bar recipe combines the flavors of chocolate, marshmallows and walnuts.

Preparation time: 10 minutes
Total time: 55 minutes
Yield: 20 servings

Ingredients
16 oz. (450 g) dark chocolate, shaved or chopped
1/2 cup (120 g) butter
1 cup (220 g) sugar
1 cup (125 g) flour
1 teaspoon (4 g) baking powder
1 teaspoon (5 ml) vanilla extract
2 (60 g) whole eggs
3/4 cup (75 g) chopped walnuts
1 cup (50 g) mini marshmallows

Method
1. Preheat your oven to 350°F and line your 9 x 13-inch baking pan with parchment paper.
2. Combine the chocolate and butter in a saucepan and cook over low heat, stir frequently until melted and smooth. Remove from heat and then transfer to a mixing bowl.

3. Add 1 cup of sugar, 1 cup of flour, baking powder, vanilla extract, and the 2 eggs. Mix well.
4. Fold in the walnuts and marshmallows until fully combined.
5. Spread this mixture into the bottom of your baking pan.
6. Place your baking pan into the oven and bake for 20 to 25 minutes. Cool in wire rack before cutting.
7. Serve and enjoy.

Nutritional Information:
Energy - 267 calories
Fat - 14.7 g
Carbohydrates - 30.9 g
Protein - 4.3 g
Sodium - 60 mg

Chocolate And Hazelnut Ice Cream

This chocolate ice cream recipe will leave you in awe at how simple and easy it is to make.

Preparation time: 30 minutes
Total time: 6 hours 30 minutes
Yield: 6 servings

Ingredients
2 1/2 cups (625 ml) whole milk
1 can (400 g) sweetened condensed milk
1/2 cup (50 g) cocoa powder
1 teaspoon (5 ml) vanilla extract
1/2 cup (60 g) hazelnuts
chocolate syrup, to serve

Method

1. Put your hazelnuts onto a baking sheet and roast it in a preheated oven set to 400°F for 10 to 15 minutes. Allow to cool for a bit, chop, then set aside.
2. Combine both milk and the cocoa powder in a blender until smooth. Transfer to a container and refrigerate for about an hour.

3. Once the cocoa mixture has been chilled, transfer it to your ice cream maker and follow the manufacturers' instructions.
4. Fold in your chopped hazelnuts then pour into a container with lid. Put it in the freezer for at least 6 hours to set.
5. Drizzle with chocolate syrup on top for more chocolate-y goodness.
6. Enjoy.

Nutritional Information:

Energy - 286 calories
Fat - 12.5 g
Carbohydrates - 37.6 g
Protein - 9.5 g
Sodium - 107 mg

Homemade Double Chocolate Ice Cream

This recipe has double the fun with the addition of chocolate chips into the creamy frozen chocolate dessert. Truly, nothing beats homemade ice cream!

Preparation time: 15 minutes
Total time: 6 hours 15 minutes
Yield: 8 servings

Ingredients
1 cup (100 g) dark chocolate, grated
1 can (400 g) sweetened condensed milk
3 tablespoons (20 g) cocoa powder
2 cups (500 ml) half and half
2 cups (500 ml) skim milk
1 teaspoon (5 ml) vanilla extract
1 cup (160 g) dark chocolate chips

Method
1. Heat the chopped semi-sweet chocolate and the condensed milk in a heavy bottomed saucepan over medium heat. Cook, stirring constantly for about 2 to 3 minutes or until the chocolate has fully melted. Remove from heat and gently add the half and half as well as the milk and vanilla extract and chocolate chips.

2. Transfer mixture into your ice cream maker and freeze it according to the manufacturers' instructions.
3. Serve and enjoy.

Nutritional Information:

Energy - 386 calories
Fat - 19.3 g
Carbohydrates - 47.9 g
Protein - 7.8 g
Sodium - 106 mg

Homemade Chocolate Chip Energy Bars

These mildly sweet bars are packed with protein and fiber. Perfect for kids snack time.
Preparation Time: 4 hours 10 minutes
Total Time: 4 hours 10 minutes
Yield: 12 servings
Ingredients
1/2 cup (130 g) cashews
1 cup (100 g) oats
1/2 cup (125 g) almond butter
1 teaspoon (5 ml) vanilla extract
1/4 cup (80 ml) maple syrup
1/3 cup (55 g) mini chocolate chips
Method
1. Line your baking pan with parchment paper. In a food processor, put our cashews and oats. Pulse them together 2 times.
2. Add the wet ingredients, namely the almond butter, vanilla extract, and maple syrup. Pulse again until everything looks moist. It should form a ball shape.
3. Fold in the chocolate chips.
4. Take your mixture and your baking pan and put the mixture firmly and evenly at the bottom of the baking pan. Cover the pan and refrigerate for 4 hours. Once set, you can cut the slab into bars.

5. Serve and enjoy.

Nutritional Information:

Energy - 173 calories
Fat - 10.1 g
Carbohydrates - 16.7 g
Protein - 3.8 g
Sodium - 2 mg

The Ultimate Chocolate Mousse

This recipe may take some time to make, but the result is definitely worth it!

Preparation time: 10 minutes
Total time: 2 hours 50 minutes
Yield: 8 servings

Ingredients
10 ounces (280 g) bittersweet chocolate, chopped
2 tablespoons (15 g) cocoa powder
4 tablespoons (60 ml) water
2 (60 g) whole eggs, separated
1 tablespoon (15 g) granulated sugar, divided
pinch of salt
1 cup (250 g) all-purpose cream

Method
1. Mix together the chocolate and cocoa powder with the water in a bowl. Place the bowl over a saucepan with some water. Heat it at a low setting so that it is just about simmering. Stir frequently. Once melted, you can remove the bowl from heat.

2. Whisk the egg yolks, the 1 1/2 teaspoons of sugar, as well as the salt in a bowl for about 30 seconds. Add the melted chocolate mixture and combine. Allow to cool for a bit.

3. Whip the egg whites until foamy. Add in the remaining sugar and whip again until stiff peaks form. Whisk in about a quarter of the egg whites into the chocolate mixture, mix thoroughly then add the remaining egg whites.
4. Whip the cream in a stand mixer on medium speed for about 30 seconds or until it starts to thicken. Increase the speed to high and whip until peaks form.
5. Fold the whipped cream into the mousse and serve in individual cups and cover with cling wrap.
6. Refrigerate for 2 hours and serve with chocolate syrup and more whipped cream on top.
7. Enjoy.

Nutritional Information:

Energy - 253 calories
Fat - 15.3 g
Carbohydrates - 24.7 g
Protein - 5.2 g
Sodium - 76 mg

Chocolate And Raspberry Mini Tarts

These lovely tarts are absolutely delicious and would surely delight everyone who eats them.
Preparation Time: 15 minutes
Total Time: 30 minutes
Yield: 16 servings
Ingredients
1 pound (450 g) pre-made tart dough or shortbread crust
4 tablespoons (60 g) unsalted butter
6 ounces (180 g) finely chopped bittersweet chocolate
1 teaspoon (2 g) strong brewed coffee
4 (60 g) whole eggs
2/3 cup (150 g) granulated sugar
1 teaspoon (5 ml) vanilla extract
1 1/2 cups (185 g) raspberries
chocolate syrup, to serve
Method
1. Preheat your oven to 425°F.
2. Divide your tart dough into 8 pieces. Put the pieces in your tart cups and put them in the freezer for about 5 minutes.
3. Place the tart cups on a baking sheet and bake them for about 5-7 minutes. Allow to cool.
4. Reduce your oven's temperature to 375°F.
5. Mix the butter with the chocolate and coffee in a saucepan. Cook over low heat for about 3 minutes.

6. In a bowl, whisk together the eggs then slowly add in the granulated sugar, chocolate mixture, and the vanilla extract. Pour and divide evenly into your tart shells.
7. Bake in the oven for about 15 minutes. Take the tarts out, allow to cool, then put the raspberries on top of each tart. You can dust them with confectioners' sugar, if desired. Drizzle with some chocolate syrup on top of the raspberries for added effect.
8. Serve and enjoy.

Nutritional Information:

Energy - 266 calories
Fat - 15.5 g
Carbohydrates - 28.6 g
Protein - 3.5 g
Sodium - 208 mg

Strawberries Dipped In Chocolate

A very delicious way to satisfy your cravings for chocolate.

Preparation Time: 10 minutes
Total Time: 10 minutes
Yield: 8 servings

Ingredients

6 ounces (180 g) dark chocolate, chopped
1/2 cup (125 g) heavy cream
2.2 pounds (1 kg) fresh strawberries

Method

1. Put your chocolate and cream in a heavy bottomed saucepan. Cook over medium heat until melted and smooth. Transfer into a small bowl.
2. Dip the tips of your strawberries into the chocolate.
3. Serve and enjoy.

Nutritional Information:

Energy - 176 calories
Fat - 9.4 g
Carbohydrates - 21.6 g
Protein - 2.5 g
Sodium - 21 mg

Delightful Chocolate Truffles

These little pieces of chocolate delights are a good gift idea for Valentine's Day.

Preparation time: 55 minutes
Total time: 55 minutes
Yield: 20 servings

Ingredients
1/2 pound (225 g) bittersweet chocolate
1/2 pound (225 g) semisweet chocolate
1 cup (250 g) heavy cream
1 teaspoon (2 g) instant coffee powder
1/2 teaspoon (2.5 ml) vanilla extract
1/2 cup (60 g) your choice of chopped nuts, optional
1/4 cup (25 g) cocoa powder

Method
1. Finely chop the chocolate and place it in a bowl.
2. Cook the heavy cream in a saucepan over medium heat until it starts to boil, stirring frequently. Remove from heat and let the cream sit for a few seconds. Pour the cream into the bowl with chocolate.
3. Using a wire whisk, stir together the chocolate and cream. The heat from the cream will slowly melt the chocolate. Continue stirring until the chocolate has melted completely.

4. Stir in the coffee, vanilla extract, and nuts. Allow this mixture to sit at room temperature for about an hour.
5. Use a teaspoon for this next step. Line a baking sheet with some parchment paper and spoon some of the chocolate mixture and form into balls and place in the baking sheet.
6. Take the balls and roll them in cocoa powder.
7. Serve the balls in mini paper cups for a nice presentation.
8. Enjoy.

Nutritional Information:
Energy - 152 calories
Fat - 10.3 g
Carbohydrates - 15.2 g
Protein - 2.2 g
Sodium - 13 mg

Chocolate And Marshmallow Fudge Bars

A perfect dessert to serve at children's parties.

Preparation time: 10 minutes
Total time: 1 hour 10 minutes
Yield: 20 servings

Ingredients
2 1/2 cups (375 ml) milk chocolate chips
1/4 cup (60 g) butter
3 cups (150 g) mini multicolored marshmallows
1 teaspoons (5 ml) pure vanilla extract

Method
1. Take your 9x9-inch baking pan and line it with parchment paper. Set aside.
2. Melt the chocolate using a double boiler or microwave. Remember to stir often! Once melted, add the vanilla and stir for a bit.
3. Fold in the marshmallows. Pour the melted chocolate mixture into the baking pan and smooth out the top. Put the baking pan in the fridge for an hour.
4. Once set, take the pan out of the fridge and cut the chocolate into small squares.
5. Serve.

Nutritional Information:
Energy - 163 calories
Fat - 9.5 g
Carbohydrates - 22.0 g
Protein - 2.0 g
Sodium - 38 mg

Classic And Easy Chocolate Pie

This super delicious chocolate pie is good way to end a family dinner.

Preparation time: 10 minutes
Total time: 4 hours 10 minutes
Yield: 12 servings

Ingredients
1 pie crust, pre-baked
1 1/2 cup (330 g) sugar
1/4 cup (25 g) cornstarch
1/4 teaspoon (1.5 g) salt
3 cups (750 ml) milk
4 (20 g) egg yolks
8 ounces (250 g) bittersweet chocolate, chopped finely
2 teaspoons (10 ml) vanilla extract
2 tablespoons (30 g) butter
whipped cream, for topping

Method
1. In a medium saucepan, stir together the sugar, cornstarch, and salt. Stir in the milk and the egg yolks. Cook over medium heat until the mixture almost comes to a boil, stirring constantly. This should take about 6 to 8 minutes. Remove from heat when it starts to bubble.

2. Add the chocolate, vanilla extract, and butter. Stir again until everything is thoroughly combined. Pour the mixture into your pie crust and chill for at least 4 hours.
3. Once set, take it out of the fridge and cut into slices. Serve with whipped cream on top.
4. Enjoy.

Nutritional Information:

Energy - 279 calories
Fat - 10.7 g
Carbohydrates - 42.6 g
Protein - 4.4 g
Sodium - 119 mg

Chocolate Pancakes

Serve your kids this amazingly delicious chocolate pancakes for your next breakfast. They will surely love it.
Preparation time: 10 minutes
Total time: 20 minutes
Yield: 6 servings

Ingredients
1 1/3 cup (165 g) flour
1/4 cup (25 g) cocoa powder
2 teaspoons (8 g) baking powder
1/4 teaspoon (1.5 g) salt
2 tablespoons (30 g) sugar
3 tablespoons (45 g) melted butter
1 teaspoon (5 ml) vanilla extract
1 1/4 cup (315 ml) milk
1 (60 g) whole egg
cooking oil spray
mixed berries, for topping
powdered sugar, for dusting

Method
1. Grease a non-stick pan with oil spray and heat over medium heat.
2. Sift all of the dry ingredients. Mix them together completely.
3. In a separate bowl, mix together the wet ingredients.

4. Make a well in the center of the dry ingredients. Pour the wet ingredient mixture into the center and combine the two mixtures together.
5. Take about 1/4 cup of the batter and put it in the pan. Cook until it bubbles then flip it over to cook the other side. Repeat procedure with the remaining batter.
6. Divide pancakes among 6 serving dishes. Top with berries and sprinkle with powdered sugar.
7. Enjoy.

Nutritional Information:

Energy - 162 calories
Fat - 6.3 g
Carbohydrates - 23.0 g
Protein - 4.7 g
Sodium - 133 mg

Easy Homemade Chocolate Crinkles

This cookie recipe is probably the simplest you can ever make!
Preparation time: 10 minutes
Total time: 25 minutes
Yield: 72 servings
Ingredients
1 cup (100 g) unsweetened cocoa powder
2 cups (440 g) white sugar
1/2 cup (125 ml) vegetable oil
4 (60 g) whole eggs
2 teaspoons (10 ml) vanilla extract
2 cups (250 g) all-purpose flour
2 teaspoons (8 g) baking powder
1/2 teaspoon (2.5 g) salt
1/2 cup (50 g) powdered sugar

Method

1. In a medium bowl, combine the cocoa, white sugar, and vegetable oil. Beat in eggs one at a time, then stir in the vanilla. Combine the flour, baking powder, and salt; stir into the cocoa mixture. Cover dough, and chill for at least 4 hours.
2. Preheat oven to 350 F. Line cookie sheets with parchment paper. Roll dough into one inch balls. I like to use a number

50 size scoop. Coat each ball in confectioners' sugar before placing onto prepared cookie sheets.
3. Bake in preheated oven for 10 to 12 minutes. Allow to cool in the cookie sheet for 2 minutes before transferring to a cooling rack.
4. Serve and enjoy.

Nutritional Information:
Energy - 58 calories
Fat - 2.0 g
Carbohydrates - 9.8 g
Protein - 0.9 g
Sodium - 34 mg

Mini Chocolate And Peanut Butter Cups

Make this yummy favorite right in your very own kitchen!

Preparation time: 1 hour
Total time: 1 hour
Yield: 24 servings

Ingredients
16 ounces (450 g) dark chocolate, melted
1 cup (250 g) peanut butter
1/4 teaspoon (1.5 g) salt
1/4 cup (25 g) powdered sugar

Method
1. Line a round tart molds with paper cups.
2. Spoon half of the melted chocolate into the cups. Fill them about halfway then spread the chocolate up the sides of the cups. Chill for about 30 minutes or until firm.
3. Mix your peanut butter together with the salt and powdered sugar in a bowl. Take your chocolate cups out of the chiller and divide the peanut butter mixture between them.
4. Spoon the remaining chocolate place it on top of the peanut butter. Chill again until firm.
5. Serve and enjoy.

Nutritional Information:

Energy - 169 calories

Fat - 11.0 g
Carbohydrates - 14.6 g
Protein - 4.1 g
Sodium - 88 mg

Chocolate Oatmeal Porridge

This porridge is best served at breakfast especially during rainy days.

Preparation time: 10 minutes
Total time: 30 minutes
Yield: 4 servings

Ingredients

1/3 cup (35 g) unsweetened cocoa powder
1 cup (250 ml) hot water
1 1/2 cups (375 ml) milk
1/4 teaspoon (1.5 g) salt
1 cup (100 g) rolled oats
2 tablespoons (30 g) brown sugar
nuts and fruit like banana, optional

Method

1. Put the cocoa powder along with the hot water in a saucepan and let it dissolve completely. Add in the milk and bring the mixture to a boil over medium heat.
2. Add in the salt as well as the oats. Simmer over low setting. Stir constantly until the oatmeal has cooked. Remove from heat then add in the honey.
3. Top with nuts and fruits of your choice.

4. Serve and enjoy.

Nutritional Information:

Energy - 157 calories
Fat - 4.2 g
Carbohydrates - 26.6 g
Protein - 7.1 g
Sodium - 122 mg

Almond And Chocolate-Covered Biscuit Sticks

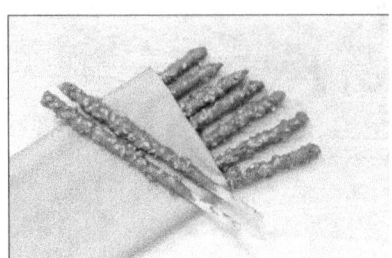

Reminiscent of Asian snacks, these biscuit sticks are very easy to make and are absolutely delicious.

Preparation time: 15 minutes
Total Time: 15 minutes
Yield: 16 servings

Ingredients
16 (40 g) plain bread sticks
1 cup (160 g) melted bittersweet chocolate chips
1/2 cup (60 g) finely chopped almonds

Method
1. Using either a microwave or a double boiler, melt your chocolate chips.
2. Add the chopped almonds and stir the mixture.
3. Dip half of your bread sticks in the mixture and put them on a parchment-lined cookie sheet to cool. Serve once set.
4. Enjoy.

Nutritional Information:
Energy - 115 calories

Fat - 5.6 g
Carbohydrates - 13.7 g
Protein - 2.6 g
Sodium - 74 mg

Chocolate Pavlova

Elegant and divine, your dinner guests would love to have this served to them.

Preparation time: 20 minutes
Total time: 2 hours 50 minutes
Yield: 12 servings

Ingredients
6 (40 g) egg whites
1/4 teaspoon (1.5 g) salt
1/4 teaspoon (0.5 g) cream of tartar
1 1/2 cups (330 g) granulated sugar
3 tablespoons (20 g) unsweetened cocoa powder
2 teaspoons (5 g) cornstarch
1 tablespoon (15 ml) vinegar
2 teaspoons (10 ml) vanilla extract
2 ounces (56 g) melted bittersweet chocolate
1 1/2 cups (375 g) whipping cream
2 teaspoons (10 g) granulated sugar
1 ounce (28 g) melted bittersweet chocolate
To Serve:
whipped cream
chocolate shavings
chocolate sauce or ganache

Method

1. Preheat your oven to 275°F.
2. Beat together the salt, cream of tartar, and egg whites. They should form soft peaks. Add in the sugar, three tablespoons at a time. Stiffer peaks should form. Sift the cocoa and the cornstarch into the mixture and stir. Lastly, add in the vanilla extract, vinegar, and melted chocolate.
3. Take your baking sheet and line it with parchment paper. Take the mixture and make a large, round shape in the center of the baking sheet. Bake for 1 1/2 hours. Take the resulting meringue from the parchment paper and transfer to a wire rack to cool completely. Should take about an hour.
4. Top with chocolate sauce, whipped cream and chocolate shavings.
5. Serve and enjoy.

Nutritional Information:
Energy - 159 calories
Fat - 3.5 g
Carbohydrates - 31.7 g
Protein - 2.7 g
Sodium - 67 mg

Banana Choco Pops

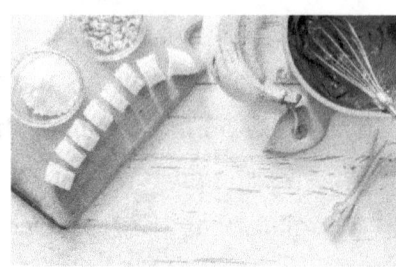

These chocolate-covered bananas taste great and fun to make!

Preparation time: 20 minutes
Total time: 2 hours 30 minutes
Yield: 12 servings

Ingredients
4 (120 g) bananas
1/4 cup (40 g) finely chopped peanuts
6 ounces (180 g) chopped dark chocolate

Method
1. Peel each banana and stick a wooden popsicle stick in each one.
2. Melt the chocolate either by microwaving it or by putting it in the top part of a double boiler. Whichever method you choose, make sure that you stir frequently. Pour the chocolate into a big bowl.
3. Dip the bananas first in chocolate then roll them in peanuts. Put the chocolate-dipped bananas in a cookie sheet lined with parchment or waxed paper.
4. Place in the freezer for about 2 hours then serve once frozen.

Nutritional Information:

Energy - 292 calories
Fat - 13.4 g
Carbohydrates - 46.3 g
Protein - 4.8 g
Sodium - 6 mg

Homemade S'mores

Relive the memories of summer camp with this delicious S'mores recipe.

Preparation time: 15 minutes
Total time: 15 minutes
Yield: 8 servings

Ingredients
8 oz. (250 g) large marshmallows
8 sheets Graham crackers (about 31 g)
8 (1 oz. or 28 g) chocolate bars

Method
1. Take a marshmallow and put it against an open flame source. It should begin to melt and turn brown. Take a graham cracker and cut it in half.
2. Put a piece of chocolate and the semi-melted marshmallow in between the two pieces of graham crackers. Repeat with remaining ingredients.
3. Serve and enjoy.

Nutritional Information:
Energy - 301 calories
Fat - 9.8 g
Carbohydrates - 49.6 g
Protein - 4.1 g
Sodium - 127 mg

Chocolate Fudge Bars

Fun and easy to make! Ask your kids to help you make these for a fun, family bonding time.

Preparation time: 15 minutes
Total time: 1 hour 15 minutes
Yield: 16 servings

Ingredients
3 cups (480 g) dark chocolate chips
1 can (400 g) sweetened condensed milk
1/4 cup (60 g) butter

Method
1. Place all three ingredients in a microwave-safe bowl. Pop them in the microwave and heat on medium setting until they start to melt together, about 2 minutes.
2. Take it out of the microwave and stir. Put it back for another heat cycle. Repeat until fully melted. Pour the mixture into an 8 x 8-inch baking pan. Chill for at least 2 hours or until set.
3. Serve and enjoy.

Nutritional Information:
Energy - 207 calories
Fat - 11 g
Carbohydrates - 28.0 g

Protein - 3.4 g
Sodium - 51 mg

Chocolate-Covered Cherry Bites

The triple C. These candies are easy to make and can be stored for more than a week.

Preparation time: 1 hour
Total time: 1 hour
Yield: 48 servings

Ingredients

4 tablespoons (60 g) softened butter
3 tablespoons (60 ml) corn syrup
1 1/2 cups (150 g) powdered sugar
48 (10 g) fresh cherries, pitted
16 ounces (450 g) melted dark chocolate

Method

1. Combine the butter and corn syrup in a bowl. Add in the powdered sugar. Knead this mixture into a soft dough. Take your cherries and cover each with dough. Chill until they are firm.
2. Dip your cherries in the melted chocolate to coat. Chill again until set.
3. Serve and enjoy.

Nutritional Information:

Energy - 80 calories
Fat - 3.8 g
Carbohydrates - 11.0 g
Protein - 0.8 g

Sodium - 8 mg

Choco Peppermint Bites

Perfect as gifts! Put them in small plastic bags and tie a twine around it. A much satisfying way to serve your candy canes.

Preparation time: 20 minutes
Total time: 2 hours 20 minutes
Yield: 16 servings

Ingredients
8 ounces (250 g) semisweet chocolate
8 ounces (250 g) white chocolate
2 tablespoons (30 ml) canola oil
1/2 teaspoon (2.5 ml) peppermint extract, divided
2 ounces (56 g) crushed peppermint candy canes
cooking oil spray

Method
1. Grease a 9 x 9-inch baking pan with oil spray and line it with wax paper.
2. Take a double boiler and put the semisweet chocolate and 1 teaspoon of canola oil in the top part. Put a simmering water underneath it and melt the chocolate. Stir frequently.
3. Once the chocolate has melted, stir in 1/4 teaspoon of the peppermint extract. Pour the melted chocolate in your baking pan and spread it evenly.
4. Refrigerate the pan until the chocolate is set.

5. Melt the white chocolate using the same process as the semisweet chocolate. Once melted, you may add the remaining 1/4 teaspoon of peppermint extract. Pour this mixture over the hardened semisweet chocolate layer and spread it evenly. Sprinkle with crushed candy canes on top. Press the candies in a little and then chill the pan again in the fridge until the chocolate has hardened.
6. Once set, take the chocolate out of the pan and cut into squares.
7. Serve and enjoy.

Nutritional Information:

Energy - 170 calories
Fat - 9.4 g
Carbohydrates - 22.9 g
Protein - 1.4 g
Sodium - 14 mg

Chocolate Bubble Tea

Make the ever-popular bubble tea right at home!

Preparation time: 10 minutes
Total time: 10 minutes
Yield: 1 serving

Ingredients
1/2 cup (125 ml) milk
1/2 cup (125 ml) freshly brewed tea
2 tablespoons (30 ml) chocolate syrup
4 tablespoons (60 g) tapioca black pearls, cooked
crushed ice, to serve

Method
1. Pour the milk, tea, chocolate syrup in a tall container with lid and shake until thoroughly combined.
2. Take a large plastic cup and put the tapioca pearls at the bottom and then pour the chocolate drink mixture all over it and serve with some crushed ice.

Nutritional Information:
Energy - 221 calories
Fat - 2.9 g
Carbohydrates - 44.3 g
Protein - 4.8 g
Sodium - 88 mg

Hot Chocolate With Marshmallows

An all-time favorite drink made with chocolate and marshmallow!

Preparation time: 10 minutes
Total time: 10 minutes
Yield: 4 servings

Ingredients
1/2 cup (50 g) unsweetened cocoa powder
a pinch of salt
1 cup (250 ml) boiling water
3 cups (750 ml) milk
1/4 cup (60 g) sugar
1/2 teaspoon (2.5 ml) vanilla extract

Method
1. Combine the cocoa powder and salt in a saucepan. Add the boiling water and bring it to a boil. Stir constantly. Reduce heat and simmer for about 2 minutes.
2. Stir in milk and sugar. Cook further 2-3 minutes or until heated through. Remove from heat then add the vanilla extract. Divide the hot chocolate among 4 cups.
3. Top with marshmallows on top.

4. Serve and enjoy.

Nutritional Information:
Energy - 165 calories
Fat - 5.2 g
Carbohydrates - 27.4 g
Protein - 8.1 g
Sodium - 129 mg

Cinnamon-Spiced Hot Chocolate

This is the perfect drink to serve during the cold season.

Preparation time: 10 minutes
Total time: 10 minutes
Yield: 4 servings

Ingredients
1/2 cup (50 g) unsweetened cocoa powder
1 cinnamon stick
1 cup (250 ml) boiling water
3 cups (750 ml) milk
1/4 cup (55 g) sugar

Method
1. Combine the cocoa powder, cinnamon stick, and boiling water in a saucepan and bring it to a boil. Stir constantly. Reduce heat and simmer for about 2 minutes.
2. Stir in milk and sugar. Cook further 2-3 minutes or until heated through. Remove from heat. Divide the hot chocolate among 4 cups.
3. Serve and enjoy.

Nutritional Information:

Energy - 164 calories
Fat - 5.2 g
Carbohydrates - 27.8 g
Protein - 8.1 g
Sodium - 90 mg

Rich Chocolate Milkshake

This fantastic drink is super easy to make and absolutely delicious!

Preparation time: 5 minutes
Total time: 5 minutes
Yield: 1 serving

Ingredients

1 scoop (60 g) chocolate ice cream
1 cup (250 ml) skim milk
2 tablespoons (40 ml) chocolate syrup
2-3 ice cubes

Method

1. Combine all of the ingredients in a blender and blend until smooth.
2. Serve in a tall glass.
3. Enjoy.

Nutritional Information:

Energy - 320 calories
Fat - 6.8 g
Carbohydrates - 52.8 g
Protein - 11.0 g
Sodium - 205 mg

Cookies And Cream Shake

The addition of chocolate cookies make this shake taste marvelous.

Preparation time: 5 minutes
Total time: 5 minutes
Yield: 2 servings

Ingredients
2 (60 g) scoops vanilla ice cream
1/2 cup (50 g) crushed oreo cookies
2 cups (500 ml) milk
3-4 ice cubes

Method
1. Blend all of the ingredients in a blender for about 2 minutes.
2. Pour into 2 tall glasses. Garnish with cookies on top, if desired.
3. Serve and enjoy.

Nutritional Information:

Energy - 339 calories
Fat - 15.5 g
Carbohydrates - 40.5 g
Protein - 10.8 g
Sodium - 238 mg

Chocolate And Vanilla Smoothie

Classy and delicious! Garnish this with vanilla pods to make a very simple, but beautiful presentation.

Preparation time: 5 minutes
Total time: 5 minutes
Yield: 2 servings

Ingredients
4 tablespoons (80 ml) chocolate syrup
1 cup (250 g) vanilla yogurt
1 cup (250 ml) whole milk
1/2 teaspoon (2.5 ml) vanilla
4-5 ice cubes
vanilla pods, for garnish
chocolate shavings, for garnish

Method
1. Blend all the ingredients together until smooth.
2. Pour in 2 chilled tall glasses and garnish with vanilla pods and chocolate shavings.

Nutritional Information:

Energy - 230 calories
Fat - 4.3 g
Carbohydrates - 33.1 g
Protein - 11.6 g
Sodium - 164 mg

Chocolate And Banana Smoothie

Delicious and filling! Kids love it and so will you!
Preparation Time: 5 minutes
Total Time: 5 minutes
Yield: 2 servings

Ingredients
1 medium (125 g) banana, cut into small pieces
2 tablespoons (40 ml) chocolate syrup
1 cup (250 ml) milk
2-3 ice cubes

Method
1. Blend all the ingredients together in a blender until smooth.
2. Pour in a chilled tall glass. Garnish with fresh mint and chocolate shavings if desired.
    3. Enjoy.

Nutritional Information:

Energy - 332 calories
Fat - 5.8 g
Carbohydrates - 63.4 g
Protein - 10.1 g
Sodium - 147 mg

White Chocolate Mocha Drink

This creamy, refreshing drink is the perfect combination of white chocolate and coffee.

Preparation time: 5 minutes
Total time: 5 minutes
Yield: 2 servings

Ingredients
2 (1 oz. or 28 ml) shots espresso coffee
4 tablespoons (80 ml) white chocolate syrup
16 ounces (450 ml) of milk
6 ice cubes

Method
1. Combine the espresso, white chocolate syrup, and milk in a blender. Process until smooth.
2. Pour into 2 chilled glasses. Add some crushed ice.
3. Serve and enjoy.

Nutritional Information:
Energy - 227 calories
Fat - 5.8 g
Carbohydrates - 34.9 g
Protein - 9.3 g
Sodium - 149 mg

Chocolate Almond Tea Latte

Scrumptious and easy to make! Perfect when you're craving for cafe-style lattes.

Preparation time: 5 minutes
Total time: 5 minutes
Yield: 2 servings

Ingredients
2 (2 g) English breakfast tea bags
2 cups (500 ml) hot water
1 cup (250 ml) almond milk
1/4 cup (80 ml) chocolate syrup
shaved chocolate (for garnish)

Method
1. Prepare the tea using the tea bags and hot water. Allow to steep for 5 minutes (less if you don't want it to be that strong).
2. Add the almond milk and chocolate syrup. Stir until combined well.
3. Divide among 2 glasses. Garnish with chocolate shavings.

Nutritional Information:
Energy - 181 calories
Fat - 4.7 g

Carbohydrates - 26.2 g
Protein - 7.4 g
Sodium - 126 mg

Caramel Hot Chocolate

The sweetness of caramel sauce blends perfectly with the chocolate flavor.
Preparation Time: 10 minutes
Total Time: 10 minutes
Yield: 2 servings
Ingredients
2 tablespoons (15 g) unsweetened cocoa powder
1/2 cup (125 ml) hot water
2 teaspoons (10 g) brown sugar
1 1/2 cups (375 ml) skim milk
2 tablespoons (40 ml) caramel sauce
Method
1. In a small saucepan, mix together the cocoa powder, hot water, and the sugar. Stir until dissolved completely.
2. Add the milk. Cook, stirring constantly over medium heat until heated through about 3 minutes.
3. Stir in caramel sauce. Pour in 2 serving cups.
4. Serve and enjoy.

Nutritional Information:

Energy - 140 calories
Fat - 0.4 g
Carbohydrates - 28.0 g

Protein - 6.8 g
Sodium - 171 mg

www.ingramcontent.com/pod-product-compliance
Lightning Source LLC
Chambersburg PA
CBHW071442070526
44578CB00001B/194